Journey of Self-Discovery: Gita's Life Lessons in Stories

JIGNESH SAPRA

Published by JIGNESH SAPRA, 2023.

While every precaution has been taken in the preparation of this book, the publisher assumes no responsibility for errors or omissions, or for damages resulting from the use of the information contained herein.

JOURNEY OF SELF-DISCOVERY: GITA'S LIFE LESSONS IN STORIES

First edition. July 29, 2023.

ISBN: 979-8223050094

Written by JIGNESH SAPRA.

To my beloved wife, **Drishti**,

You are the vision that brings clarity to my life, the guiding light that leads me through every chapter. This book is a testament to the love and inspiration you bring to my writing journey. Thank you for being my constant support and my most cherished muse.

With all my love, Jignesh

The Seeker of Serenity

"There is neither this world nor the world beyond. Happiness for the person who has been able to control their mind, renouncing all material desires, and living free from desires and attachment."

Once upon a time, in a bustling kingdom, there lived a young prince named Arjun. He was known for his intelligence, charisma, and remarkable fighting skills. Despite having everything a prince could desire, Arjun felt an inexplicable emptiness within him.

One day, while wandering through the palace gardens, Arjun overheard a group of wise sages conversing about the path to true happiness and inner peace. Intrigued, he approached them and asked for guidance. The sages spoke of renouncing material desires and attachments and controlling the mind to find genuine contentment.

Inspired by their words, Arjun decided to embark on a journey to seek inner fulfillment. He bid farewell to his kingdom and set out on a quest to find the elusive happiness he yearned for.

As he traveled across lands and encountered various challenges, Arjun faced temptations that tested his commitment to his newfound quest. Along the way, he met an enigmatic hermit named Krishnan, who seemed to have a tranquil aura about him.

Curious, Arjun approached the hermit and sought his wisdom. Krishnan welcomed Arjun with a warm smile and said, "Happiness lies not in worldly possessions or fleeting desires, but in the mastery of one's own mind. Detach yourself from the material world, and you will find lasting contentment."

Intrigued by Krishnan's serene demeanor, Arjun became his devoted disciple, eager to learn the secrets of true happiness. Krishnan taught Arjun various meditation techniques and spiritual practices to tame the restless mind and cultivate inner peace.

As months passed, Arjun diligently practiced what he learned from Krishnan. He began to feel a profound change within himself. The once tumultuous thoughts in his mind began to subside, and a newfound sense of calm enveloped him.

With Krishnan's guidance, Arjun learned to detach himself from material desires, focusing instead on selfless service and kindness towards others. He discovered that happiness was not dependent on external circumstances but originated from within.

One day, while meditating under a majestic banyan tree, Arjun experienced a profound realization. He understood that the world as we perceive it is transient and filled with dualities of joy and sorrow. True happiness, he concluded, could only be found by transcending these dualities through inner detachment.

Arjun's newfound wisdom and inner transformation became renowned throughout the kingdom. People from far and wide sought his counsel on the pursuit of happiness and inner peace. He shared the teachings he had learned from Krishnan, inspiring others to embark on their own journeys of self-discovery.

Over time, Arjun's kingdom underwent a remarkable change. It became a haven of peace and prosperity, where the people valued contentment and compassion over material possessions.

As the years passed, Arjun continued to live a life of simplicity and spiritual wisdom, serving as a beacon of hope for those seeking true happiness. He had learned that happiness lay not in possessions, but in the mastery of one's mind, renouncing all material desires, and living with detachment and selflessness.

And so, the tale of the Seeker of Serenity, Prince Arjun, and his journey to find true happiness became a timeless legend, reminding people for generations to come that genuine contentment could only be found within themselves.

The Weaver of Destiny

"You have control over doing your respective duty only, but no control or claim over the results."

In a quaint village nestled amidst rolling hills and lush greenery, lived a skilled and hardworking weaver named Ravi. Ravi was known for his exceptional craftsmanship, weaving intricate and beautiful fabrics that enchanted everyone who laid eyes on them.

One day, as Ravi sat in his loom, his young apprentice, Amar, approached him with a troubled expression. Amar admired Ravi's talent and wanted to be just as successful. However, he often felt disheartened when his efforts didn't yield the same results as his master's.

"Master Ravi," Amar said with a hint of frustration, "I don't understand. I put in as much effort as you do, but my weavings never turn out as exquisite as yours."

Ravi looked at Amar kindly and smiled. "Amar, my young apprentice," he said, "you must understand that you have control over doing your respective duty, which is weaving. But remember, you have no control over the results. Weaving, like life, is a tapestry of uncertainties, and we must learn to embrace both success and failure."

Amar looked puzzled, but Ravi continued to impart his wisdom. "You see, my dear apprentice, life is like a loom. We each have a role to play, a duty to fulfill. You must focus on weaving to the best of your ability, without being attached to the outcome. Embrace each thread, each moment, and weave with dedication and love."

Ravi's words resonated with Amar, and from that day onward, he approached his work with a newfound perspective. Instead of fixating on the product, he immersed himself in the creative process, finding joy in every intricate pattern he weaved.

One day, as the village prepared for a grand festival, Ravi and Amar were tasked with creating a stunning tapestry to adorn the center stage. The weavers worked tirelessly, pouring their hearts into the project.

Finally, the day of the festival arrived, and the villagers marveled at the beautiful tapestry. The vibrant colors and exquisite design left everyone spellbound. Amar felt a sense of fulfillment like never before, realizing that he had indeed mastered the art of focusing on his duty rather than the outcome.

However, the true test of Ravi's wisdom came when a sudden storm unexpectedly swept through the village. Despite their efforts to protect the tapestry, raindrops fell, smudging the colors and muddying the fabric.

Amar felt devastated, but Ravi remained remarkably composed. "Amar, remember what I told you, "he said calmly. "We have control over our actions, but the results are beyond our grasp. Let us repair the tapestry to the best of our abilities and accept what comes."

Together, they mended the damaged sections, and, to their surprise, the tapestry took on a new, weathered beauty. The imperfections added character, reminding them of the unpredictable nature of life.

As the villagers admired the tapestry, Ravi and Amar realized the profound truth in their master's words. Life was a journey of weaving, where they must pour their heart and soul into their respective duties, and yet, the results would often be beyond their control.

From that day forward, Ravi and Amar continued to weave with dedication and passion, embracing both the joys and challenges that life presented. They understood that while they were the weavers of their destiny, they could only control their actions, not the outcomes. And in this realization, they found contentment and peace, living harmoniously with the ebb and flow of life's tapestry.

The Karma's Guardian

"*No one who does good work will ever come to a bad end, either here or in the world to come.*"

In a picturesque village nestled amid lush green fields and blooming flowers, lived a kind-hearted and hardworking man named Anand. Known for his unwavering commitment to helping others, Anand spent his days selflessly assisting his fellow villagers with any task they needed, no matter how big or small.

One day, a wandering sage named Yogi arrived in the village. As the news spread, the villagers gathered to seek the sage's blessings and wisdom. Intrigued by Yogi's serene presence, Anand approached him and bowed respectfully.

"Great Sage," Anand said, "I am humbled by your presence. Is there any advice you can give me to lead a life of purpose and fulfillment?"

Yogi smiled warmly at Anand and replied, "Dear one, you already possess the key to a life well-lived. Your good deeds and selfless actions will protect you both in this world and the world to come."

Anand felt a sense of reassurance and continued with his compassionate deeds, nurturing a deep understanding that karma, the law of cause and effect, would always safeguard those who dedicated themselves to good work.

In time, Anand's reputation as the "Karma's Guardian" spread far and wide. He became a guiding light for others, inspiring them to embrace acts of kindness and service to humanity.

However, not everyone in the village shared Anand's benevolent nature. There was a group of envious individuals who disapproved of Anand's growing influence and goodwill.

One day, the jealous villagers devised a malicious plan to tarnish Anand's reputation. They spread false rumors about him, attempting to paint his good deeds as self-serving and deceitful.

As the rumors reached Anand's ears, he felt a pang of hurt and sadness. But remembering Yogi's words, he chose not to be deterred by the slander and continued to focus on his virtuous path.

Meanwhile, the village chief, Maharaj, heard of the rumors and the ensuing turmoil. He decided to investigate the matter impartially, seeking the truth behind the accusations.

As Maharaj delved deeper into the situation, he witnessed firsthand the impact of Anand's kind actions. He noticed how Anand's efforts had uplifted the entire village and improved the lives of its inhabitants.

Moved by the overwhelming evidence of Anand's goodness, Maharaj called for a village assembly. In front of the entire community, Maharaj cleared the air, exposing the deceitful intentions of those who sought to harm Anand's reputation.

In the light of truth, the villagers realized the extent of Anand's selflessness, and they offered heartfelt apologies for having doubted him.

From that day on, Anand's influence grew even stronger. He remained true to his path, undeterred by the challenges and obstacles that came his way. The village prospered under the guidance of the Karma's Guardian, and harmony and happiness became the norm.

As years passed, Anand's earthly journey came to an end, and he transcended to the world beyond. The villagers mourned his departure, but they knew that his legacy would live on in their hearts.

In the world to come, Anand's soul found eternal peace, as his good deeds had earned him the rewards of a life well-lived. His unwavering commitment to doing good work had guided him through both the trials of this world and the world beyond.

And so, the tale of Anand, the Karma's Guardian, became a timeless story of how goodness, compassion, and selflessness protect and guide those who walk the path of righteousness.

The Serenity of the Wise

"*The awakened sages call a person wise when all their undertakings are free from anxiety about results.*"

In the ancient city of Ayur, there lived a humble and contemplative man named Siddharth. From a young age, Siddharth was known for his profound wisdom and clarity of thought. He possessed a deep understanding of life's mysteries and had a unique way of finding tranquility in every situation.

People from neighboring towns and villages sought Siddharth's counsel, hoping to gain insight into their own dilemmas. His wisdom seemed boundless, and his advice always resonated with truth and compassion.

One day, a group of curious seekers approached Siddharth and asked him, "O Wise One, how do you manage to remain so serene and undisturbed amidst the challenges of life?"

Siddharth smiled gently and replied, "My dear friends, the secret to inner peace lies in freeing ourselves from anxiety about the results of our undertakings. When we detach from the outcomes and focus on the present moment, we find true wisdom."

Intrigued by his words, the seekers requested Siddharth to elaborate further. He began to share a parable that conveyed the essence of his teachings:

"In a distant village, there lived a skilled potter named Kavi. He was renowned for his exquisite craftsmanship and beautifully crafted pottery. Every piece he created was a masterpiece, admired by all who saw them.

One day, a curious traveler passing through the village approached Kavi and said, 'I have heard of your talent, Master Potter. Can you teach me your art?'

Kavi smiled warmly and agreed to mentor the traveler. He showed him the techniques and secrets of pottery, but he also shared a crucial lesson, 'While you shape the clay with skill and dedication, remember that the outcome lies beyond your control. Embrace the process but release your attachment to the results.'

The traveler diligently practiced under Kavi's guidance, but he struggled to let go of his attachment to the end products. He would often worry about whether people would admire his pottery as they did Kavi's.

Observing the traveler's anxiety, Kavi gently advised, 'Worrying about the outcomes hinders your ability to create from the heart. True mastery comes from dedicating yourself to the present moment and infusing love and passion into your craft.'

The traveler realized the wisdom in Kavi's words and decided to follow his advice. He immersed himself in the creative process, savoring each moment of shaping the clay, regardless of the result.

With time, the traveler's pottery began to exude a unique aura of peace and serenity. Each piece he crafted carried a sense of contentment and joy that touched the hearts of those who beheld them.

Upon seeing the transformation in the traveler's work, Kavi smiled and said, 'Now you understand the essence of wisdom. When you free yourself from anxiety about the results, you find freedom in every endeavor.'

The traveler thanked Kavi wholeheartedly for his invaluable lesson. He realized that wisdom lay not in achieving perfection or garnering praise, but in the joy of creation itself.

And so, the traveler returned to his own village, embodying the teachings of the wise potter. He became known for his serene nature and ability to find peace in every undertaking.

In the city of Ayur, Siddharth concluded the parable, leaving the seekers with a profound lesson. "Just like the potter, when we focus on the present, infusing love and dedication into our actions, we become wise. The awakened sages recognize wisdom in those whose hearts are free from anxiety about the results of their endeavors."

From that day forth, the seekers, inspired by Siddharth's wisdom, embraced a new perspective on life. They began to find solace in the process of living, knowing that true wisdom lay in cherishing each moment, free from anxiety about the outcomes. And in their newfound serenity, they discovered the essence of true enlightenment.

The Battle Within

"**A** *person is his own friend as well as his own enemy."*
In the ancient kingdom of Rajapur, there lived a young and ambitious warrior named Arjun. He possessed exceptional skills with the sword and bow, and his determination to be the greatest warrior in the realm knew no bounds.

Arjun's prowess in battle earned him numerous accolades and admiration from fellow warriors and citizens alike. However, beneath his brave exterior, Arjun struggled with a constant internal conflict. He was torn between his desire for greatness and his fear of failure.

One evening, as the sun set over the majestic Rajapur palace, Arjun sought solace by the serene lake. Lost in his thoughts, he heard a gentle voice whispering to him, "A person is his own friend as well as his own enemy."

Confused by the enigmatic words, Arjun looked around, but there was no one in sight. He wondered if it was his own mind playing tricks on him. Nevertheless, the words lingered, and he couldn't dismiss them.

That night, as Arjun lay in his chamber, he reflected on the mysterious message. The more he contemplated, the more he realized its profound meaning. He began to understand that he was indeed his own friend and enemy.

His desire for greatness and perfection drove him to excel in battle, but it also brought forth a fear of failure, haunting him like a relentless enemy. He understood that his inner conflicts were hindering his true potential, preventing him from achieving the greatness he sought.

Determined to confront his inner demons, Arjun sought the counsel of the kingdom's wise sage, Guru Dev. He poured his heart out, confessing his struggles and fears.

Guru Dev listened attentively, then spoke, "Arjun, the battles we face within ourselves are often the fiercest. The mind can be our greatest ally or our most formidable foe. It is essential to recognize your fears and doubts and learn to control your thoughts."

He continued, "Embrace your aspirations, but do not let the fear of failure consume you. Instead, use it as a driving force to improve and grow. Remember, true strength lies not only in defeating external adversaries but also in conquering the battles within."

Arjun was deeply moved by Guru Dev's wisdom and realized that he needed to master his own mind. He began a rigorous practice of meditation and introspection, seeking to understand the root of his fears and doubts.

As weeks turned into months, Arjun's mind became calmer and more focused. He learned to silence the inner critic that had been holding him back. With each passing day, he felt a newfound sense of control over his emotions and thoughts.

Arjun's transformation did not go unnoticed. On the day of the annual Kingdom Tournament, he entered the arena with newfound confidence and self-assurance. His swordplay was impeccable, and his archery skills were unmatched.

As he faced his opponents, Arjun felt no fear or doubt, for he had become his own ally, supporting and encouraging himself. He emerged victorious, not only in the tournament but also in the battle within.

The people of Rajapur marveled at the transformation in their once-conflicted warrior. They had witnessed a profound change in Arjun's demeanor and understood the significance of being one's own friend.

From that day on, Arjun lived by the sage's wisdom, embracing his desires and fears, knowing that he held the power to be his own ally or enemy. He continued to grow as a warrior and as a person, understanding that true greatness lies in mastering oneself.

And so, the tale of Arjun, the warrior who conquered the battles within, became a timeless reminder that the mind can be both friend and enemy, and the key to greatness lies in learning to be a true friend to oneself.

The Virtuous Weaver

"*A person's own duty, even if imperfectly performed, is better than doing another person's duty well.*"

In a quaint village nestled amidst emerald fields, there lived a skilled weaver named Dev. He was known for his intricate tapestries and beautiful fabrics that adorned the homes of the villagers.

One day, as Dev sat at his loom, a renowned painter named Anika visited the village. Anika had heard of Dev's exceptional craftsmanship and was eager to witness it firsthand. She approached Dev and said, "I have admired your work from afar, dear weaver. Would you allow me to observe your artistry?"

Dev warmly welcomed Anika and invited her to watch him work. As Anika observed the rhythmic dance of threads on the loom, she was mesmerized by Dev's skill and dedication.

Impressed by Dev's talent, Anika couldn't help but compare her own work as a painter to his craft. She confided in him, "Your tapestries are awe-inspiring, Dev. I often wonder if my paintings can evoke the same emotions in people."

Dev smiled gently and replied, "Anika, we are both artists, but our paths are different. Each of us has our unique duty, and it is essential to honor and focus on our own craft, regardless of imperfections."

Anika pondered his words and realized the truth in them. She understood that comparing her work with Dev's was futile, as they had distinct styles and mediums of expression.

As days passed, Anika spent more time with Dev, learning about his life and values. She admired his dedication to his art and the genuine joy he found in weaving. Dev, in turn, appreciated Anika's passion for painting and the stories she conveyed through her art.

One day, the village decided to hold an art fair to celebrate the creativity of its residents. Both Dev and Anika were invited to showcase their work. Excitement buzzed in the air as villagers eagerly awaited the exhibition.

On the day of the fair, Dev displayed his intricate tapestries, and Anika showcased her vivid paintings. As the visitors admired their works, Anika couldn't help but feel a pang of insecurity. She feared her paintings wouldn't be appreciated as much as Dev's exquisite weavings.

Sensing Anika's unease, Dev approached her with a reassuring smile. "Anika, remember our conversation. Your duty as a painter is to create from your heart, not to worry about comparisons. Each of us brings something unique to the world, and that is the beauty of art."

Encouraged by Dev's words, Anika found solace in her duty as a painter. She let go of her self-doubt and embraced the joy of creating with her own distinct style.

As the art fair continued, Dev's tapestries and Anika's paintings received admiration from the villagers. Each piece of art evoked different emotions, and the visitors appreciated the beauty and uniqueness of both crafts.

In the end, both Dev and Anika felt a deep sense of contentment in fulfilling their own duties. Dev was grateful for the opportunity to weave beautiful tapestries, while Anika relished the joy of painting stories on canvas.

The villagers celebrated the harmony and humility of the two artists, recognizing that each person's duty, when done with dedication and passion, holds its own significance.

From that day on, Dev and Anika continued to pursue their art, recognizing the wisdom in Dev's words: "A person's own duty, even if imperfectly performed, is better than doing another person's duty well." They found fulfillment in honoring their unique callings and appreciated the beauty that each art form brought to the world.

And so, the tale of Dev, the virtuous weaver, and Anika, the passionate painter, became a timeless reminder of the importance of embracing one's own duty and celebrating the uniqueness of every individual's contribution to the tapestry of life.

The Serenity of the Mind

"**O**ne who has control over the mind is tranquil in heat and cold, in pleasure and pain, and in honor and dishonor."

In the serene mountains of Himalaya, there lived a wise and tranquil monk named Ashwin. He was revered by people far and wide for his unwavering composure and peaceful demeanor, even in the face of life's harshest challenges.

One day, a young seeker named Ravi traveled from a distant village to seek Ashwin's guidance. Ravi had heard tales of the monk's profound wisdom and sought to understand the secret to his inner tranquility.

As Ravi approached the humble abode of the monk, he noticed Ashwin sitting calmly under the shade of a banyan tree. The monk's face bore a serene smile, and his eyes reflected profound peace.

"Master Ashwin," Ravi greeted with respect, "I have traveled far to seek your wisdom. How do you remain so tranquil amidst the changing tides of life?"

Ashwin's eyes twinkled with kindness as he replied, "My dear seeker, the secret lies in mastering the mind. One who has control over the mind is not affected by external circumstances. They remain tranquil in the face of heat and cold, pleasure and pain, and honor and dishonor."

Intrigued, Ravi asked, "But how does one attain such mastery over the mind?"

Ashwin patted the ground beside him, inviting Ravi to sit. He began to share his wisdom:

"The mind is like a wild horse, untamed and restless. It wanders in all directions, chasing desires and reacting to external stimuli. To control the mind, one must first observe it without judgment. Watch the thoughts come and go like passing clouds in the sky."

Ravi listened intently as Ashwin continued, "Through regular practice of meditation and mindfulness, you will gradually gain control over the mind. You will learn to detach from the external world, finding tranquility within."

"Does this mean one becomes indifferent to the world?" Ravi asked.

"No, my dear seeker," Ashwin replied gently. "Control over the mind does not imply indifference. It means that you remain balanced and centered, unaffected by the dualities of life. Just as a lotus bloom untainted in muddy waters, you can maintain inner serenity amidst life's challenges."

Eager to learn, Ravi spent days under Ashwin's guidance, diligently practicing meditation and mindfulness. With each passing day, he felt a newfound sense of peace and control over his thoughts and emotions.

As the seasons changed, Ravi observed Ashwin's tranquility remaining unwavering. Whether it was the scorching heat of summer or the biting cold of winter, the monk remained undisturbed, content in his inner sanctuary.

Ravi marveled at the monk's equanimity and said, "Master Ashwin, I have learned much from you, but I fear that I may falter when I return to the bustling world outside."

Ashwin smiled warmly, "Remember, my dear seeker, that mastering the mind is a continuous journey. Even if you stumble along the way, do not be disheartened. Each moment is an opportunity to renew your commitment to inner peace."

With a heart full of gratitude, Ravi bid farewell to Ashwin and returned to his village. He continued to practice what he had learned, and over time, he too found greater tranquility amidst life's challenges.

From that day on, Ravi understood the profound truth in Ashwin's words: "One who has control over the mind is tranquil in heat and cold, in pleasure and pain, and in honor and dishonor." The seeker had discovered the secret to true peace—the mastery of one's own mind.

And so, the tale of Ashwin, the serene monk, and Ravi, the devoted seeker, became a timeless reminder that the mind holds the key to inner tranquility and that through mindful practice, one can find solace amidst life's ever-changing landscape.

The Liberation of Detachment

"*Those who are motivated only by desire for the fruits of action are miserable, for they are constantly anxious about the results of what they do.*"

In the bustling city of Karmaville, there lived a young and ambitious man named Aryan. He was known for his intelligence and unwavering determination to achieve success in every endeavor he pursued. Aryan was convinced that the key to happiness lay in accumulating wealth, fame, and recognition.

One day, while strolling through the city's vibrant marketplace, Aryan overheard a group of wise sages discussing the nature of happiness and contentment. Intrigued, he approached them and inquired about the secret to true fulfillment.

The eldest sage, Gandhar, smiled gently at Aryan and said, "Young man, the pursuit of success and prosperity can be a path filled with misery and anxiety if it is driven solely by the desire for the fruits of your actions."

Perplexed, Aryan asked, "But isn't the desire for success a natural and necessary motivation to achieve greatness?"

Gandhar nodded and replied, "Desire, indeed, can be a driving force, but when it becomes the sole focus, it leads to constant worry and disappointment. The key lies in performing your actions with dedication and excellence, without being attached to the outcomes."

Aryan was taken aback by the sage's response. The concept of detachment from the results of his actions was foreign to him. He had always believed that success and happiness were synonymous with the achievements he could boast about.

With a hint of skepticism, Aryan asked, "How can one find contentment if not through the fruits of their labor?"

Gandhar, with infinite wisdom, shared a parable to illustrate his point:

"In a nearby village, there lived a skilled farmer named Keshav. He tended to his fields with utmost care, sowing seeds and nurturing the crops. Keshav knew that his duty was to give his best to the land, but he did not let the anticipation of the harvest consume him.

As the crops grew, the weather took an unexpected turn, and a severe storm threatened to destroy all of Keshav's hard work. In the face of uncertainty, he remained calm and focused on protecting the crops, without being overly anxious about the outcome.

When the storm passed, Keshav's fields stood resilient, and his harvest was bountiful. He was content, not because of the abundance of his yield, but because he had performed his duty with dedication and detachment."

Listening to the parable, Aryan began to understand the profound lesson within. He realized that his constant anxiety about achieving specific results had hindered his ability to enjoy the journey of his pursuits fully.

With newfound clarity, Aryan decided to embrace the path of detachment in his endeavors. He channeled his energies into his work, enjoying each step of the process without being consumed by the result.

As days turned into months, Aryan's approach yielded remarkable results. He found a deep sense of contentment in the pursuit of his goals, irrespective of the outcomes. He became free from the shackles of constant worry and anxiety, finding joy in the very act of doing.

As word spread of Aryan's transformation, people sought his counsel on finding fulfillment in their own lives. He shared the wisdom he had gained from the sages of Karmaville, inspiring others to embrace the path of detachment.

And so, the tale of Aryan's liberation from the desire for the fruits of action became a timeless reminder that true happiness lies not in the outcomes we seek, but in the dedication, passion, and detachment we bring to each endeavor. By focusing on the journey, rather than the destination, we find contentment and freedom from the burden of constant anxiety.

The Blissful Soul

"*The soul who meditates on the Self is content to serve the Self and rests satisfied within the Self.*"

In the tranquil village of Serenity Grove, there lived a gentle and introspective soul named Maya. She was known for her serene demeanor and her profound love for meditation and self-discovery.

Maya's days were spent in quiet contemplation, seeking to understand the depths of her being. She believed that true contentment could only be found within oneself, and so, she dedicated herself to the practice of meditation on the Self.

As the sun dipped below the horizon, bathing the village in a warm glow, Maya would find her favorite spot under a blossoming cherry tree. There, amidst the melodious chirping of birds and the rustling of leaves, she would delve deep into the realms of her soul.

One evening, as Maya sat in meditation, she experienced a profound revelation. Self, she realized, was not separate from the world around her. It was a boundless ocean of consciousness, where all beings were connected in an intricate web of existence.

With each breath, Maya felt an overwhelming sense of contentment filling her heart. She understood that the key to inner peace lay in serving the Self and embracing the interconnectedness of all life.

From that day on, Maya dedicated herself to a life of selfless service. She tended to the needs of her fellow villagers, offering a helping hand to those in distress and spreading love and kindness wherever she went.

People noticed the transformation in Maya's presence. Her mere presence seemed to radiate a calming energy, and her acts of service touched the hearts of many.

One day, a weary traveler passing through Serenity Grove sought refuge in the village. Exhausted from his journey, he approached Maya, hoping for a place to rest.

Without hesitation, Maya offered him shelter and nourishing food. As they sat together, the traveler gazed at Maya's serene countenance and asked, "How do you maintain such tranquility amidst life's uncertainties?"

Maya smiled gently and replied, "I have learned that the true path to contentment lies in serving the Self—the interconnected essence that flows within all beings. When we serve others, we serve ourselves, for we are all connected in this vast tapestry of existence."

The traveler was deeply moved by Maya's words and the serenity that enveloped her. He decided to stay in Serenity Grove for a while, seeking to understand the profound wisdom that had transformed Maya's life.

Under Maya's guidance, the traveler learned the art of meditation on the Self. He realized that true contentment could be found within, by serving others with a compassionate heart.

As days turned into weeks, the traveler's heart blossomed with gratitude for the lessons he had learned. He felt a newfound sense of contentment and fulfillment, knowing that he could rest satisfied within the Self, regardless of external circumstances.

With a heart full of gratitude, the traveler bid farewell to Serenity Grove, carrying the profound teachings of Maya with him. He understood that the soul who meditates on the Self finds contentment in selfless service, resting peacefully within the vast ocean of interconnected consciousness.

And so, the tale of Maya, the blissful soul, and the wandering traveler became a timeless reminder that true contentment is not found in external pursuits, but within the depths of our being. By serving others with love and compassion, we find fulfillment and rest satisfied within the vastness of the Self.

The Steady Flame

"*When meditation is mastered, the mind is unwavering like the flame of a lamp in a windless place.*"

In the sacred city of Dhyanapur, nestled amidst serene mountains, lived a dedicated young seeker named Arav. From a tender age, Arav had been drawn to the path of meditation, seeking to tame the restless waves of his mind and uncover the depths of inner peace.

Under the guidance of Guru Devi, a wise and revered teacher, Arav immersed himself in the practice of meditation. With unwavering determination, he sat for hours, learning to still the fluctuations of his thoughts and emotions.

One evening, as the sun dipped below the horizon, Guru Devi summoned Arav for a special discourse. Seated under the tranquil shade of a banyan tree, she spoke with a gentle smile, "Arav, when meditation is mastered, the mind becomes as unwavering as the flame of a lamp in a windless place."

Intrigued, Arav asked, "But Guru Devi, my mind still wanders during meditation. How can I attain such steadiness?"

Guru Devi replied, "Like the flame of a lamp, the mind flickers in response to the winds of desires, worries, and distractions. But with persistent practice, you can anchor your focus on the present moment, just as a lamp's flame remains steady in a windless abode."

Determined to attain mastery over meditation, Arav diligently followed his teacher's guidance. He practiced daily, observing the ebb and flow of his thoughts with patient acceptance.

As weeks turned into months, Arav's meditative practice deepened. He discovered that by surrendering to the present moment, his mind became more resilient and focused.

One day, as the gentle breeze rustled the leaves of the banyan tree, Guru Devi invited Arav to join her in meditation. Together, they sat in silence, their minds intertwining in the realm of stillness.

As Arav immersed himself in the depth of his being, he felt an inner calmness like never before. The distractions that had once stirred his mind seemed distant and inconsequential.

In that moment of clarity, Arav realized that he had become one with the present moment. Like the unwavering flame of a lamp, his mind rested serenely, untouched by the winds of restlessness.

With a heart full of gratitude, Arav opened his eyes, smiling at Guru Devi. "I have experienced the stillness you spoke of, Guru Devi," he said. "My mind was like the steady flame of a lamp, unaffected by the winds of distraction."

Guru Devi nodded approvingly. "You have glimpsed the essence of meditation, my dear seeker. Just as the flame remains unwavering in a windless place, your mind finds stability when it rests in the present moment."

From that day on, Arav continued to deepen his meditation practice, savoring the moments of stillness within. He understood that the key to mastering meditation was not to suppress his thoughts, but to observe them with gentle awareness.

The village of Dhyanapur noticed the transformation in Arav's presence. His aura exuded a sense of calm and clarity that touched the hearts of all who encountered him.

With his mind now like the steady flame of a lamp, Arav became a beacon of peace for the village. He shared the wisdom of meditation with those willing to learn, guiding them on the path to inner serenity.

And so, the tale of Arav, the seeker with the unwavering mind, and Guru Devi, the wise teacher, became a timeless reminder that through meditation, the mind finds its steadiness, akin to the flame of a lamp in a windless place. With patient practice and self-awareness, we too can uncover the profound stillness that lies within our being.

The Path of Steady Wisdom

"*A person can achieve steady wisdom when they renounce all desires for sense gratification.*"

In the ancient kingdom of Serenica, there lived a young and ambitious scholar named Rishi. He had a thirst for knowledge and an insatiable desire for recognition and worldly success. Rishi believed that the key to happiness and wisdom lay in amassing wealth, fame, and accolades.

One day, while wandering through the royal gardens, Rishi chanced upon a group of venerable sages engaged in a profound discussion. Intrigued, he approached them and asked, "Honored sages, how does one attain steady wisdom?"

The eldest sage, Sage Vidyut, smiled warmly and replied, "Wisdom comes to a person when they renounce all desires for sense gratification. Detachment from the allure of worldly pleasures allows the mind to find stillness and clarity."

Rishi was taken aback by the sage's response. Renouncing desires for sense gratification seemed like an impossible feat to him. However, intrigued by the idea of acquiring steady wisdom, he decided to seek the guidance of Sage Vidyut.

Under the sage's tutelage, Rishi learned about the art of detachment and self-discipline. Sage Vidyut taught him the importance of taming the mind's incessant desires and cravings, leading it towards inner calm and tranquility.

As Rishi delved deeper into the teachings, he realized that his desires were akin to wild horses, pulling him in various directions, leaving him restless and unfocused. He understood that true wisdom could only arise from a mind free from the shackles of desires.

Determined to attain steady wisdom, Rishi began practicing self-control and renunciation. He gradually let go of the material pursuits that had once consumed him. Instead, he immersed himself in the pursuit of knowledge for its own sake, without the desire for recognition or rewards.

As Rishi progressed on this path, his mind found a newfound stillness. The inner turmoil he had once experienced began to dissipate, making way for clarity and wisdom to emerge.

One day, the kingdom of Serenica faced a grave crisis, and the king sought counsel from the wisest minds in the land. Among the sages summoned was Rishi, whose reputation for steady wisdom had spread far and wide.

As Rishi stood before the king and his courtiers, he spoke with a serene confidence. His counsel was not clouded by personal desires or ambitions but was solely driven by the pursuit of truth and the well-being of the kingdom.

The king and his advisors were impressed by Rishi's wisdom and sagacity. They followed his counsel, and the crisis was averted successfully.

As word of Rishi's steady wisdom reached all corners of the kingdom, people sought his guidance on matters of importance. Rishi became a trusted advisor and a symbol of wisdom for the people of Serenica.

Through his journey of renouncing desires for sense gratification, Rishi had discovered the true essence of wisdom. He understood that wisdom was not about accumulating external accomplishments but about finding inner peace and contentment.

The path of steady wisdom transformed Rishi's life, and he devoted himself to serving the kingdom and its people with selflessness and compassion.

And so, the tale of Rishi's journey to steady wisdom and the guidance of Sage Vidyut became a timeless reminder that when one renounces desires for sense gratification, the mind attains clarity and tranquility. Through the pursuit of inner calm and selflessness, one unlocks the doors to true wisdom and becomes a guiding light for others on the path of righteousness.

The Dual Nature of the Mind

"*A person should elevate themselves by their mind, and not degrade themselves. The mind is their friend, and also their enemy.*"

In the vibrant town of Uplifta, there lived a young and ambitious individual named Kavya. Blessed with intelligence and determination, Kavya dreamt of achieving great heights in life. However, she often found herself battling the conflicting forces within her mind.

One day, Kavya sought the counsel of the esteemed philosopher, Master Varun. She confided in him about her inner struggles and asked, "Master Varun, how can I elevate myself and reach my full potential, when my mind seems to pull me in opposite directions?"

Master Varun smiled knowingly and replied, "Kavya, the mind is a powerful force that can either elevate you to great heights or drag you down. It is both your friend and your enemy, depending on how you wield its power."

Intrigued, Kavya asked, "But how can I control my mind and make it my ally on the path to success?"

Master Varun shared a parable to illustrate the dual nature of the mind:

"Imagine there are two companions who accompany you on your journey. One is a wise and kind friend, always guiding you with good intentions. The other is mischievous and impulsive, leading you astray with temptations and distractions. These two companions are your own thoughts—the friend is positive and uplifting, while the enemy is negative and degrading."

Kavya nodded, understanding the analogy. Master Varun continued, "To elevate yourself, you must nurture the positive aspects of your mind and quiet the negative ones. Cultivate thoughts of self-belief, determination, and resilience. These thoughts will propel you towards your goals and uplift your spirit."

Kavya reflected on Master Varun's words, realizing that she had often been a victim of her own negative thoughts. She decided to take charge of her mind, making a conscious effort to focus on uplifting and encouraging thoughts.

In the following weeks, Kavya practiced mindfulness and self-awareness. Whenever negative thoughts arose, she gently acknowledged them and redirected her focus towards positive affirmations.

As she began to elevate her mind, Kavya noticed a significant change in her outlook and actions. She felt more confident, and her decision-making became more astute. She was now forging a path towards her dreams with a clear and determined mind.

Master Varun observed Kavya's transformation with pride. He knew that she had understood the profound lesson about the mind's duality. However, he also recognized that the battle was not won yet.

He reminded Kavya, "Remember, my dear, the mind's nature is fluid. Just as a river's course can change, your thoughts can waver. Keep vigilant and continue to elevate yourself with positivity."

Kavya nodded, grateful for the guidance. She knew that nurturing her mind would be an ongoing journey. But with determination and the wisdom she had gained, she felt equipped to face any challenge.

As the years passed, Kavya's success and growth became a testament to the power of a mind uplifted. She remained committed to cultivating her thoughts and ensuring her mind remained her most potent ally.

And so, the tale of Kavya's journey to elevate her mind and Master Varun's wisdom became a timeless reminder that a person's mind can be both friend and enemy. By nurturing positive thoughts and maintaining self-awareness, one can harness the mind's potential for elevation and transcendence. In mastering the art of the mind, Kavya discovered the key to unlocking her true potential and achieving greatness in life.

The Power of Action

"*Perform your obligatory duty, because action is indeed better than inaction.*" In the bustling city of Dutifuland, there lived a young and conscientious individual named Ananya. She was diligent and responsible, always eager to fulfill her duties with sincerity and dedication.

One day, as Ananya sat by the serene riverbank, she overheard a wise sage imparting his wisdom to a group of seekers. Intrigued, she approached them and listened intently to the sage's teachings.

The sage spoke, "Perform your obligatory duty, for action is indeed better than inaction. The path of responsibility and purposeful action leads to growth and fulfillment."

Ananya nodded in agreement, but a question lingered in her mind. She asked the sage, "But what if one's actions don't seem to make a significant impact or bring about the desired results?"

The sage smiled gently and replied, "The true essence of action lies not merely in its immediate outcomes but in the dedication and intention with which it is carried out. Every action, no matter how small, contributes to the larger tapestry of life."

The sage's words resonated with Ananya, and she realized that her pursuit of perfection sometimes led her to doubt the value of her actions. She understood that true fulfillment lay in embracing her duties wholeheartedly, without being attached to the results.

Inspired by the sage's wisdom, Ananya returned to her daily life with a newfound perspective. She diligently fulfilled her obligations, whether it was in her professional work or her personal relationships, without worrying about the outcomes.

As days turned into weeks, Ananya noticed a transformation within herself. Her sense of fulfillment and contentment grew, knowing that she was doing her best in every situation.

One day, Ananya encountered a group of underprivileged children who were struggling to access education. The sight deeply moved her, and she felt a sense of responsibility to make a difference in their lives.

Ananya volunteered her time and resources, setting up a makeshift classroom and providing the children with basic educational materials. She poured her heart into teaching them, encouraging them to dream big and work hard.

Months passed, and Ananya noticed remarkable progress in the children. Their enthusiasm for learning had grown, and their eyes gleamed with newfound hope and ambition.

However, as Ananya immersed herself in her work, doubts began to surface. She wondered if her efforts were enough to create a lasting impact or if she should do more.

One evening, she sought the counsel of the wise sage once again. With a heavy heart, she confessed her uncertainty.

The sage listened attentively, then spoke, "Ananya, remember that action is indeed better than inaction. Your dedication to these children's education has already made a positive difference in their lives. The impact of your actions may not always be immediately evident, but trust that every effort counts."

The sage's words reassured Ananya, and she felt a renewed sense of purpose and determination. She continued her work with unwavering commitment, knowing that her actions were sowing the seeds of positive change.

As the years passed, Ananya's small classroom grew into a thriving educational center, uplifting the lives of countless underprivileged children. She had become a beacon of hope and inspiration for the community, all through the power of action.

And so, the tale of Ananya's journey to embrace the power of action and the wisdom of the sage became a timeless reminder that performing one's obligatory duty, with dedication and intention, leads to growth and fulfillment. In embracing the path of responsibility and purposeful action, Ananya discovered the true essence of making a meaningful difference in the lives of others.

The Eternal Rhythm of Life

"*The nonpermanent appearance of happiness and distress, and their disappearance in due course, are like the appearance and disappearance of winter and summer seasons.*"

In a quaint village nestled amidst rolling hills, lived a wise old storyteller named Amar. With a gentle smile and twinkling eyes, he would captivate the villagers with his tales of life's profound truths.

One evening, as the sun set, casting a golden hue over the village, Amar gathered the villagers under the ancient banyan tree. He began weaving a tale that held a profound message about the impermanence of life.

"Listen closely, my dear friends," Amar began, "for I shall share a tale of the eternal rhythm of life."

He narrated the story of a young farmer named Rohan, who lived by the banks of a river. Rohan was content with his simple life, finding joy in the changing seasons that nature bestowed upon him.

As the tale unfolded, Amar said, "The nonpermanent appearance of happiness and distress, and their disappearance in due course, are like the appearance and disappearance of winter and summer seasons."

He explained that just as winter brings its biting cold and summer its scorching heat, life too presents its share of joys and sorrows. Seasons change, and so do the circumstances of life. Happiness and distress are transient, like the fleeting moments of a passing season.

Rohan's life, like the river's flowing current, experienced various ebbs and flows. During bountiful harvests, he reveled in the happiness of abundance. Yet, when harsh weather struck, he faced distress and uncertainty. Through it all, he maintained an unwavering acceptance of life's impermanence.

One day, a wandering sage arrived in the village. Intrigued by the sage's wisdom, Rohan sought his counsel on finding lasting happiness.

The sage smiled gently and said, "Young man, just as the river flows, life too flows in its ever-changing course. Happiness and distress are mere waves in the vast ocean of existence. Embrace them without attachment, for they are transient."

With these words, the sage imparted a profound teaching to Rohan. He understood that the key to lasting happiness lay in accepting the impermanence of life's joys and sorrows.

As years passed, Rohan lived his life in harmony with the wisdom he had received. He faced challenges with resilience, knowing that like the seasons, they too would pass. He cherished moments of joy, savoring them with gratitude while recognizing their fleeting nature.

The villagers noticed the profound transformation in Rohan's outlook on life. He had become a beacon of peace and contentment, radiating a serene aura that touched everyone he encountered.

Through the seasons of life, Rohan remained steadfast, like the river flowing with the rhythm of nature. His understanding of life's impermanence had set him free from the chains of attachment and aversion.

And so, the tale of Amar's story about the eternal rhythm of life became a timeless reminder of the impermanence of happiness and distress. Just as winter and summer seasons come and go, life's moments of joy and sorrow appear and disappear. Embracing this truth with grace, like Rohan, allows one to dance harmoniously with the eternal rhythm of life.

The Dance of Change

"*Change is the law of the universe. You can be a millionaire, or a pauper in an instant.*"

In the heart of a bustling city, there resided an ambitious and hardworking man named Vikram. With dreams of prosperity and success, he dedicated his days to climbing the corporate ladder, striving for financial abundance.

One fateful evening, as Vikram walked through the city streets, he stumbled upon an old bookstore tucked away in a quiet alley. Intrigued, he entered the dimly lit store, drawn to the antiquated wisdom that adorned its shelves.

Amongst the dusty tomes, he discovered a weathered book with a mysterious title: "The Dance of Change." Curiosity piqued, he opened its pages and began to read the timeless tale it held within.

The book recounted the story of a wealthy merchant named Rajan, whose life revolved around the pursuit of riches. He relished his opulent lifestyle, believing it would shield him from the uncertainties of life.

One day, a wandering sage crossed paths with Rajan and sensed the burdens the merchant carried. The sage, named Yogi, spoke, "Change is the law of the universe, my friend. You can be a millionaire, or a pauper, in an instant."

Perplexed, Rajan asked, "But how can I protect myself from the sudden twists of fate?"

Yogi replied, "True security lies not in the accumulation of wealth, but in embracing the impermanence of life. Instead of clinging to your riches, cultivate qualities like humility, compassion, and detachment. They will anchor you amidst the storms of change."

As Vikram read the tale, he realized the resonance it held with his own life. He, too, had sought security in material wealth, believing it would shield him from the uncertainties of the world.

Intrigued by the sage's wisdom, Rajan set aside his relentless pursuit of riches and sought to cultivate humility and compassion. He engaged in acts of selfless service, reaching out to those less fortunate and sharing his wealth with those in need.

As Vikram immersed himself in the story, he felt a stirring within his soul. He saw his own reflection in Rajan, recognizing the impermanence of his worldly pursuits.

Vikram closed the book and left the bookstore with a newfound perspective. He realized that change was inevitable, and his fortunes could transform in the blink of an eye.

Instead of living in fear of sudden change, Vikram decided to embrace the impermanence of life. He redirected his focus towards not only achieving financial success but also nurturing his relationships and cherishing moments of joy and connection.

As the years passed, Vikram's life encountered various ups and downs, just as the seasons of change unfurled around him. Through it all, he faced each shift with resilience and grace, knowing that true security resided in the richness of his character and the love he shared with others.

With a heart that had learned to dance with change, Vikram found peace amidst life's uncertainties. He no longer defined his worth by material possessions but by the richness of his soul.

And so, the tale of "The Dance of Change" became a timeless reminder that change is the law of the universe. Like Rajan, Vikram, and all those who come to understand this truth, one can find security not in fleeting wealth but in the enduring qualities of the heart. Embracing the dance of change, they journey through life's uncertainties with courage, compassion, and an unshakable spirit.

The Ocean of Tranquility

"One who is not disturbed by the incessant flow of desires—that enter like rivers into the ocean, which is ever being filled but is always still—can alone achieve peace, and not the person who strives to satisfy such desires."

In a serene coastal village, there lived a wise elder named Guruji, whose profound teachings were sought after by many seeking inner peace. His words held the wisdom of ages, and people from far and wide would travel to hear him speak.

One day, amidst the gentle lapping of waves on the shore, a curious young seeker named Lina approached Guruji. She expressed her desire to find peace amidst the incessant flow of desires that seemed to disturb her mind.

Guruji smiled warmly and began to share his wisdom, "Lina, desires are like rivers that flow ceaselessly into the vast ocean of the mind. They seek fulfillment, but the ocean remains ever still, always filled yet undisturbed."

Perplexed, Lina asked, "But how can I find peace amidst the constant influx of desires? Should I not strive to fulfill them?"

Guruji replied, "Peace is not found in the fulfillment of desires, for their satisfaction only leads to temporary contentment. True peace lies in becoming the serene ocean that embraces the flow of desires without being agitated."

To illustrate his point, Guruji led Lina to the seashore, where they gazed at the expansive ocean stretching into the horizon. "Observe the ocean, Lina," Guruji said. "Despite the countless rivers that pour into it, it remains calm and tranquil. The key lies in accepting desires without being attached to their outcomes."

Lina contemplated Guruji's words, realizing that her struggles with desires stemmed from the attachment to their fulfillment. She understood that the pursuit of external satisfaction could never lead to lasting peace.

With Guruji's guidance, Lina began to practice mindfulness and self-awareness. She observed her desires arising like ripples on the surface of her mind, but instead of indulging them, she let them flow like rivers into the vast ocean of her consciousness.

As days turned into weeks, Lina experienced a newfound sense of peace within herself. She learned to distinguish between genuine needs and fleeting desires. By embracing her desires with detachment, she freed herself from the turmoil of constant craving.

One evening, Lina returned to Guruji, her eyes shining with inner clarity. "I have begun to experience the ocean of tranquility within me," she said. "Instead of being disturbed by my desires, I am learning to let them flow without clinging to their fulfillment."

Guruji smiled, his heart filled with joy for his young disciple. "You have understood the essence of peace, my dear Lina," he said. "In becoming the ocean, you find the freedom to navigate the rivers of desires without losing your serenity."

As Lina continued her journey, she shared Guruji's teachings with others, spreading the wisdom of finding peace amidst the tumult of desires. Her presence became a source of solace for those seeking to quell the storms within their minds.

And so, the tale of Lina's quest for peace and Guruji's guidance became a timeless reminder that true tranquility is found in becoming the serene ocean, accepting desires without attachment. Like the vast ocean, one can embrace the continuous flow of desires without being disturbed, thereby discovering the profound peace that resides within.

Taming the Restless Mind

"The mind is restless and difficult to restrain, but it is subdued by practice."
In the heart of an ancient forest, there lived a contemplative hermit named Siddharth. With an aura of tranquility, he had dedicated his life to the pursuit of inner peace and wisdom. Many seekers sought his guidance on the path to mastering the mind.

Among those who sought Siddharth's wisdom was a young traveler named Aria. Restless and seeking solace from the chaos of the world, Aria approached the hermit with a heart heavy with questions.

"Siddharth," Aria implored, "my mind is a tempest of thoughts and emotions. It seems impossible to restrain its relentless restlessness. How can I find stillness amidst this storm?"

The hermit gazed at Aria with gentle eyes and spoke, "The mind is indeed like a restless wind, forever wandering and challenging to restrain. But remember, it is through dedicated practice that the mind can be subdued."

Intrigued, Aria asked, "What kind of practice can grant me the serenity I seek?"

Siddharth responded, "Practice begins with self-awareness. Observe the ceaseless currents of thoughts flowing within you without judgment. Be a witness to their movement, acknowledging them without being carried away by their waves."

Aria nodded, eager to learn more. She spent days under Siddharth's guidance, delving into the art of mindfulness and meditation. With each passing moment, she learned to watch her thoughts and emotions without being swept away by them.

As the weeks turned into months, Aria's practice deepened. Siddharth taught her the power of conscious breathing, the art of grounding oneself in the present moment, and the beauty of embracing impermanence.

One day, Aria experienced a moment of profound clarity. As she sat in meditation, a strong surge of restlessness engulfed her mind. Instead of resisting, she followed Siddharth's guidance and observed the storm of thoughts passing through her consciousness.

With each breath, the restless winds of her mind began to subside. Like a tempest transforming into a gentle breeze, her thoughts gradually settled, and she found herself anchored in a newfound stillness.

When Aria shared her experience with Siddharth, he smiled warmly. "You have glimpsed the power of practice," he said. "The mind, once wild and untamed, can be calmed through consistent effort and self-awareness."

Encouraged by her progress, Aria continued her daily practice with dedication. She realized that the key to subduing the restless mind lay not in forceful restraint, but in gentle observation and patience.

As the seasons changed, Aria's mind underwent a profound transformation. It became a serene lake, reflecting the beauty of the present moment without being disturbed by the ripples of thoughts and emotions.

With a heart overflowing with gratitude, Aria bid farewell to Siddharth, knowing that her journey to mastering the mind was ongoing. She left the forest with newfound strength and resilience, equipped to navigate life's challenges with an anchored mind.

And so, the tale of Aria's quest for stillness and Siddharth's wisdom became a timeless reminder that while the mind may be restless and challenging to restrain, dedicated practice and self-awareness hold the key to its subjugation. By observing the currents of thoughts without judgment, one can find the serenity that resides within, like a calm lake undisturbed by the turbulence of the world.

The Divine Instrument

"The power of God is with you at all times; through the activities of mind, senses, breathing, and emotions; and is constantly doing all the work using you as a mere instrument."

In a quaint village nestled amidst lush greenery, there lived a humble farmer named Keshav. He toiled under the sun's warm embrace, tending to his crops with unwavering dedication. Keshav was known for his deep faith in the divine and his belief that God's presence was ever-present.

One day, a traveler passing through the village heard about Keshav's unwavering devotion and sought to learn from him. Intrigued, the traveler approached Keshav and asked, "How do you maintain such unwavering faith in God?"

Keshav smiled warmly and replied, "The power of God is with me at all times, guiding my every action. Whether it is tilling the soil, sowing seeds, or reaping the harvest, I am but an instrument in the divine symphony."

The traveler was curious to know more and asked, "But how do you perceive God's presence in your everyday activities?"

Keshav explained, "God's presence is not confined to places of worship or prayer. It permeates every aspect of creation, including the activities of the mind, senses, breathing, and emotions. With every breath I take, I feel the divine energy flowing through me, empowering me to carry out my duties with love and devotion."

The traveler pondered Keshav's words and decided to stay in the village for a while, learning from the farmer's deep wisdom.

As days turned into weeks, the traveler observed Keshav's way of life. He noticed that the farmer approached his daily tasks with a sense of surrender, offering each action as a divine offering.

One evening, as the sun dipped below the horizon, the traveler sat with Keshav under the vast expanse of the starlit sky. "Tell me more about being an instrument of God," the traveler requested.

Keshav looked up at the twinkling stars and said, "Just as the stars shine brightly, playing their part in the cosmic dance, I too play my role in the grand tapestry of creation. God's power flows through me, guiding my hands and heart in harmony with the rhythms of life."

The traveler marveled at Keshav's profound connection with the divine. He realized that God's power was not distant or elusive but ever-present, entwined with every heartbeat and every breath.

As the traveler continued to learn from Keshav, his perspective on life began to shift. He embraced the idea of being a divine instrument, allowing the power of God to work through him in all endeavors.

When it was time for the traveler to bid farewell to the village, he thanked Keshav for the invaluable teachings. "You have shown me the true essence of faith and surrender," the traveler said. "Through your example, I have learned to trust in the divine plan and embrace life as a sacred dance."

Keshav smiled; his heart filled with joy. "Remember, my friend," he said, "God's power is always with you. In every moment, in every breath, and in every action, you are an instrument of the divine."

With newfound wisdom in his heart, the traveler embarked on his journey, carrying the timeless teachings of being a divine instrument wherever he went.

And so, the tale of Keshav, the humble farmer, and the traveler's quest for understanding became a timeless reminder that the power of God is ever-present within us. As we surrender to the divine flow, we become instruments through which God's work is accomplished, making our every action a sacred offering in the symphony of creation.

The Journey of the Soul

"*You came empty-handed, and you will leave empty-handed.*"
In a quaint mountain village, nestled amidst nature's splendor, there lived a venerable sage named Anand. Known for his profound wisdom, people from far and wide sought his counsel on matters of life and existence.

One day, a curious traveler named Arjun arrived in the village. Drawn by the tales of the sage's insight, Arjun sought an audience with Anand.

As they sat under the shade of a towering banyan tree, Arjun posed a question, "Wise Anand, what is the essence of life? What should one strive for in this ephemeral existence?"

Anand smiled gently and replied, "Dear traveler, the essence of life lies not in accumulating worldly possessions but in recognizing the transient nature of our journey. Remember, you came empty-handed into this world, and you will leave empty-handed."

Intrigued, Arjun asked, "Does this mean that we should not strive for success or prosperity?"

Anand explained, "Striving for success and prosperity is not inherently wrong, but they should not become the sole purpose of our existence. Material possessions are like passing clouds, appearing and disappearing with the winds of time."

Arjun pondered the sage's words, realizing the truth in his teachings. He had witnessed the impermanence of life in various forms—the fleeting beauty of a blooming flower, the changing colors of the sky at sunset, and the ever-shifting seasons.

"Then what should be the focus of our journey?" Arjun inquired.

Anand replied, "Focus on the growth of your soul. Cultivate virtues like compassion, love, kindness, and selflessness. Let your actions be guided by the higher purpose of serving others and making the world a better place."

Arjun reflected on the sage's words, understanding that true fulfillment came from the expansion of the soul rather than the accumulation of possessions.

As days turned into weeks, Arjun immersed himself in the village community, engaging in acts of service and spreading kindness wherever he went. He found joy in simple acts of sharing and giving without expecting anything in return.

With each passing day, Arjun's heart felt lighter, and he experienced a sense of peace he had never known before. He had embraced the wisdom of the sage and understood that his true journey lay in the growth of his soul.

One evening, as the sun painted the sky with hues of gold and orange, Arjun returned to Anand to express his gratitude. "Thank you for showing me the path of the soul," he said. "I now understand that our time in this world is fleeting, and it is the growth of the soul that truly matters."

Anand smiled, his eyes reflecting the wisdom of ages. "May you continue to walk the path of the soul with love and compassion," he said. "Remember that the journey of life is a sacred dance between the eternal and the ephemeral."

As Arjun bid farewell to the sage and the village, he carried the timeless teachings in his heart. He understood that in this transient existence, what truly mattered was not what one gathered along the way, but the depth and richness of the soul's journey.

And so, the tale of Arjun's encounter with the sage Anand became a timeless reminder that we all come empty-handed into this world, and we will leave empty-handed. The true essence of life lies not in material possessions but in the growth of the soul and the impact we leave on others as we journey through this ephemeral existence.

The Path to Devotion

"A *person cannot achieve devotion without controlling their mind."*
In the heart of a bustling city, there lived a curious and devoted young woman named Maya. Drawn to the teachings of spiritual masters, she longed to experience true devotion in her heart.

One day, Maya heard about a renowned guru, Swami Vishal, who was known for his profound wisdom on matters of the soul. Determined to seek his guidance, she embarked on a journey to his humble ashram situated amidst serene hills.

As Maya approached the ashram gates, she felt a sense of reverence in her heart. The ashram's tranquil atmosphere seemed to whisper the promise of profound insights within.

Upon meeting Swami Vishal, Maya shared her desire to cultivate unwavering devotion in her heart. "Dear Swami," she asked, "how can I achieve true devotion?"

Swami Vishal smiled kindly and replied, "Devotion is not a mere sentiment, Maya. It is a deep connection with the divine that can only be attained through a controlled and focused mind."

Perplexed, Maya inquired, "But how can I control my mind? It seems to wander endlessly, pulled in different directions."

Swami Vishal nodded understandingly and explained, "The mind is like a restless monkey, jumping from thought to thought. To cultivate devotion, you must first learn to tame this monkey mind."

He continued, "Begin by observing your thoughts without judgment. Just as a watchful observer, witness the thoughts that arise and let them pass without getting entangled in their drama. With practice, you will learn to steer your mind towards the path of devotion."

Maya took Swami Vishal's teachings to heart and began her daily practice of meditation and self-awareness. As days turned into weeks, she noticed a gradual change in her mind's temperament. The once restless monkey began to sit still for longer moments, allowing her to delve deeper into the realm of devotion.

As her practice deepened, Maya found solace in the stillness of her mind. It was in this quietude that she felt the presence of the divine, permeating every fiber of her being.

One evening, after a particularly profound meditation session, Maya sought Swami Vishal's guidance once more. "Swami," she said, "I have experienced moments of profound devotion during my practice. But how do I carry this devotion into my daily life?"

Swami Vishal smiled, his eyes reflecting the radiance of the soul. "Devotion is not confined to the ashram or the meditation cushion," he replied. "It is in how you conduct yourself in the world, with love, compassion, and kindness towards all beings. Carry the essence of your meditative devotion in every action, and you will experience the divine in everything you do."

As months passed, Maya's devotion expanded beyond the confines of her practice. She infused her daily life with love and compassion, seeing the divine in every face she encountered.

With every act of kindness, Maya realized that her controlled mind had become a channel for the divine to flow through her. She had achieved the essence of devotion through the taming of her restless mind.

And so, the tale of Maya's journey to devotion and Swami Vishal's wisdom became a timeless reminder that a person cannot achieve devotion without controlling their mind. In taming the restless monkey mind, one opens the door to the divine presence within, cultivating true devotion that permeates every aspect of life.

The Serenity of Duty

"*P*erform *your duty with a calm mind, without attachment to success or failure.*"

In the ancient city of Ayodhya, there lived a diligent and devoted young man named Ravi. He was known for his unwavering commitment to his duties as a royal scribe, transcribing important decrees and preserving the kingdom's history.

One day, as Ravi diligently worked on a manuscript, he overheard a group of scholars discussing the teachings of a wise sage who had recently visited the city.

Intrigued by the sage's profound wisdom, Ravi sought an audience with him. The sage, named Guruji, welcomed him with a warm smile.

"Guruji," Ravi asked, "how can I excel in my duties and find contentment amidst life's challenges?"

Guruji replied, "Perform your duty with a calm mind, without attachment to success or failure. Let your actions be guided by duty alone, and do not be swayed by the outcomes."

Curious to understand more, Ravi questioned, "But should I not strive for success and recognition in my work?"

Guruji explained, "It is natural to desire success, but when you become overly attached to the results, you risk losing your peace of mind. The key is to offer your best effort and let go of the attachment to the fruits of your actions."

As Ravi pondered Guruji's words, he realized the wisdom they held. He had often found himself anxious and worried about the results of his work, fearing failure or seeking praise.

Determined to practice Guruji's teachings, Ravi returned to his duties with a newfound perspective. He approached each task with a calm mind, focusing solely on fulfilling his responsibilities to the best of his abilities.

As days turned into weeks, Ravi experienced a transformation within himself. With the burden of attachment lifted, he found a deep sense of serenity in his work. He took joy in the process of writing, finding contentment in the act of serving the kingdom with dedication.

One evening, as the sun set over Ayodhya, Ravi approached Guruji once again. "Your teachings have brought me a sense of peace and fulfillment," he said with gratitude. "I have learned to perform my duty with a calm mind, embracing the process rather than being consumed by the outcomes."

Guruji smiled, his eyes reflecting the depth of his wisdom. "You have understood the essence of true contentment," he said. "When you perform your duty with detachment, you remain unaffected by success or failure. This inner calm becomes your guiding light, leading you to the path of excellence."

With Guruji's guidance, Ravi continued to practice the art of performing his duty with a serene mind. He became known not only for his exceptional work but also for the tranquility he brought to every task.

As the years passed, Ravi's dedication and calm demeanor earned him the respect of the kingdom's people and the appreciation of the royal family.

And so, the tale of Ravi's journey to finding serenity in duty and Guruji's wisdom became a timeless reminder that true fulfillment lies in performing one's duty with a calm mind, free from the chains of attachment to success or failure. By embracing the process and offering one's best efforts, one finds contentment in the journey itself, shining brightly like a steady flame amidst life's ever-changing tides.

The Mind's Tempest

"*The mind is restless, turbulent, obstinate, and very strong, O Krishna, and to subdue it, I think, is more difficult than controlling the wind.*"

On the sacred battlefield of Kurukshetra, the noble prince Arjuna stood with his charioteer and divine guide, Lord Krishna. As the battle drums echoed, Arjuna confided in Krishna, revealing the turmoil within his heart.

"O Krishna," Arjuna began, "my mind is restless, turbulent, and obstinate. It is as strong as the mightiest wind, and I find it difficult to control. How can I subdue this tempest within me?"

With infinite compassion in his eyes, Lord Krishna smiled and responded, "Indeed, Arjuna, the mind is restless and fierce like the untamed wind. But with perseverance and practice, it can be harnessed."

Krishna began to impart timeless wisdom to his dear friend, "Just as a seasoned sailor learns to navigate through rough seas, you must learn to tame the waves of your mind. The mind can be your best friend or your worst enemy—it all depends on how you choose to discipline it."

Arjuna listened attentively as Krishna continued, "The mind is influenced by desires, attachments, and external circumstances. It wanders like an unbridled horse, taking you on unexpected journeys. But with awareness and self-discipline, you can bring it back to the path of righteousness."

Krishna encouraged Arjuna to practice meditation and mindfulness, to observe the thoughts that arose without getting swept away by their force. He reminded him that thoughts were like passing clouds; they would come and go, but his true self was like the vast sky, unaffected by their transience.

As the lessons from Krishna sank deep into Arjuna's heart, he realized that controlling the mind required continuous effort, just like taming the mighty wind. But he also understood that it was a journey worth undertaking, for the peace and clarity it would bring.

With Krishna's guidance, Arjuna embarked on his inner quest, seeking to subdue the restless mind. In moments of turmoil, he reminded himself of the divine wisdom he had received, and with each breath, he practiced being present in the moment.

As the days turned into weeks and the weeks into months, Arjuna's efforts bore fruit. Though the mind would sometimes resist, he developed the strength to bring it back to focus. He found solace in the stillness within, as the winds of restlessness gradually subsided.

One day, while sitting with Krishna, Arjuna expressed his gratitude for the invaluable teachings. "O Krishna," he said, "your wisdom has become the guiding light in my life. By taming my mind, I have found peace and clarity even amidst life's challenges."

Krishna smiled, acknowledging Arjuna's progress, and said, "The mind can be an ally when it is under your control. Remember, dear friend, the journey of self-mastery is ongoing, and each step you take brings you closer to the true nature of your being."

And so, the tale of Arjuna's inner journey and Krishna's divine guidance became a timeless reminder that the mind, like the wild wind, can be challenging to control. But with perseverance, self-awareness, and dedication, one can find the strength to tame the tempest within and discover the boundless peace that resides in the depths of the soul.

The Ocean of Inner Peace

"A person who is not disturbed by the incessant flow of desires—that enter like rivers into the ocean, which is ever being filled but is always still—can alone achieve peace, and not the person who strives to satisfy such desires."

In the heart of a bustling city, there lived a content and serene soul named Ananya. Amidst the ceaseless flow of desires and temptations around her, she remained untouched by the restless waves that engulfed many.

Curiosity led many seekers to her doorstep, seeking the secret to her unwavering peace. Among them was a young aspirant named Raman, who had heard tales of Ananya's tranquility amidst the turbulent currents of life.

Approaching Ananya with humility, Raman asked, "O wise one, how do you maintain such inner peace amidst the incessant flow of desires and distractions that surround us?"

Ananya smiled warmly and replied, "Dear seeker, imagine the mind as an ocean, and desires as rivers that flow incessantly into it. The ocean is ever being filled, but it remains still, untouched by the commotion above its surface."

Raman's curiosity deepened, and he asked, "But how can one achieve such calmness amidst the pull of desires?"

Ananya explained, "Peace is found not in satisfying every desire that arises but in understanding their transient nature. Observe the desires like passing clouds in the sky of your mind and let them drift away without attachment."

With a heart eager to learn, Raman became Ananya's disciple. He dedicated himself to the practice of mindfulness and self-awareness, guided by her timeless wisdom.

As days turned into weeks, Raman found himself growing in inner strength. The more he observed the ebb and flow of desires without being entangled, the more peace filled his heart.

Ananya taught Raman to shift his focus from external gratification to nurturing the depths of his soul. She emphasized the importance of cultivating virtues like contentment, compassion, and selflessness.

Raman began to let go of the constant need for external validation and possessions, realizing that true peace lay in accepting the natural abundance within himself.

One evening, as the sun painted the sky in hues of gold, Raman sought Ananya's guidance once again. "I am beginning to experience the peace you spoke of," he said. "The incessant flow of desires no longer disturbs my tranquility."

Ananya smiled, her eyes reflecting the wisdom of a life well-lived. "You have understood the essence of inner peace," she said. "In the depths of your soul lies a reservoir of serenity, and as long as you remain anchored there, desires can no longer toss you around like waves in a stormy sea."

As the years passed, Raman's inner peace became a beacon of hope for those seeking solace in a restless world. He shared Ananya's teachings with others, inspiring them to navigate life's currents with grace and composure.

And so, the tale of Raman's quest for inner peace and Ananya's wisdom became a timeless reminder that true tranquility is found in being undisturbed by the incessant flow of desires. Like the ocean that remains still amidst the rivers' entry, a person who cultivates inner peace finds harmony within, untouched by the transient desires that dance around them.

The Path of Authenticity

"*A person's own duty, even if imperfectly performed, is better than doing another person's duty well.*"

In a peaceful village nestled amidst lush greenery, there lived two close friends, Ravi and Keshav. Both were skilled craftsmen, but their personalities and approaches to life were vastly different.

Ravi was a dedicated potter, whose passion for clay and craftsmanship ran deep in his veins. He poured his heart and soul into every piece he created, even if they didn't always turn out perfectly.

Keshav, on the other hand, was a skilled blacksmith. He admired Ravi's pottery but couldn't resist the temptation to try his hand at it. Despite his proficiency in forging metal, he struggled to replicate Ravi's finesse in pottery.

One day, Keshav approached Ravi with a perplexed look on his face. "Ravi," he said, "I can't seem to match your skill in pottery. My creations lack the beauty and precision that yours possess."

Ravi smiled warmly and replied, "Keshav, each of us has a unique path and purpose. While you excel in blacksmithing, I find my joy in molding clay. Our duties are not meant to be compared, but to be embraced wholeheartedly."

Keshav nodded thoughtfully, but a lingering doubt remained. He admired Ravi's dedication to his craft and yearned for the same level of satisfaction in his own work.

Ravi could sense Keshav's internal struggle and shared a tale from their village's ancient lore. "In the days of old," he said, "there was a great king who desired to learn the art of archery. His guru, a master archer, guided him to focus on his own dharma—the duty of being a ruler—instead of pursuing another's path."

"In the pursuit of another's duty," Ravi continued, "the king would never reach his full potential as a leader. Similarly, in trying to excel at pottery, you might miss the beauty of your blacksmithing craft."

Keshav reflected on Ravi's words and realized the truth they held. Embracing his true calling as a blacksmith, he delved deeper into his craft, honing his skills with unwavering dedication.

Meanwhile, Ravi continued to create pottery with his heart and soul, cherishing the beauty in the imperfections that made each piece unique.

As time passed, Keshav found solace in his blacksmithing, and his creations began to carry a distinct touch that was entirely his own. He no longer felt the need to compare himself to Ravi, for he had embraced his own path and purpose.

One day, the village organized an exhibition to showcase the craftsmen's works. People marveled at Ravi's exquisite pottery and Keshav's exceptional blacksmithing. Each craftsman was celebrated for the authenticity and dedication they brought to their own duties.

As the sun set on the exhibition, Ravi and Keshav stood side by side, content with the knowledge that they had found fulfillment by following their true callings.

And so, the tale of Ravi and Keshav became a timeless reminder that a person's own duty, even if imperfectly performed, is better than doing another person's duty well. Embracing one's authentic path brings a sense of purpose and joy that cannot be matched by comparison or imitation. Everyone has a unique contribution to make, and the world thrives when everyone follows their true calling with dedication and authenticity.

The Three Gates of Self-Destructive Hell

*"L*ust, anger, and greed are the three gates to self-destructive hell."*
In a distant kingdom, there lived a wise and compassionate sage named Devan. He was revered for his profound understanding of human nature and the paths that led to both suffering and liberation.

One day, a troubled young man named Raj approached the sage, burdened by the turmoil within him. He confessed, "O wise Devan, I find myself constantly trapped in the clutches of destructive emotions—lust, anger, and greed. They seem to lead me towards a path of darkness and despair. How can I free myself from their grip?"

Devan's eyes held a gentle understanding as he replied, "My son, you have discovered the three gates to self-destructive hell, and you have taken the first step towards liberation by acknowledging their presence. Let me guide you on a path of inner transformation."

With Raj as his eager disciple, Devan began to share the wisdom of the ages, rooted in ancient scriptures and the insights of enlightened beings.

"Lust," Devan began, "is a fire that burns relentlessly, consuming the very essence of our being. To conquer lust, one must cultivate self-control and discernment. Recognize the transient nature of desires and turn your focus towards pursuits that elevate the spirit."

Raj listened intently, determined to break free from the chains of lust that bound him.

"Anger," Devan continued, "is a storm that clouds the mind, obscuring the light of reason and compassion. To tame anger, one must practice patience and forgiveness. Respond to challenging situations with understanding and calmness, knowing that anger only begets more suffering."

Raj nodded, absorbing the sage's teachings like a thirsty soul in a desert.

"Greed," Devan added, "is a voracious beast that can never be satisfied. To overcome greed, one must embrace contentment and gratitude. Appreciate the abundance that life offers and share your blessings with others, for true wealth lies not in possessions but in the richness of the heart."

As Raj immersed himself in Devan's teachings, he began to observe the arising of lust, anger, and greed within himself. With practice and guidance, he learned to recognize their destructive nature and respond with wisdom and restraint.

Days turned into weeks, and weeks into months. Gradually, Raj felt the grip of these self-destructive emotions loosen, replaced by a newfound sense of peace and clarity.

One day, as the sun dipped below the horizon, Raj returned to Devan with a smile on his face. "Master," he said, "your wisdom has led me to a place of inner freedom. I have learned to navigate the treacherous gates of lust, anger, and greed, and their hold on me has weakened."

Devan smiled, proud of his disciple's progress. "You have embarked on the path of self-mastery," he said, "and your commitment to inner transformation will lead you to liberation from suffering."

With Devan's guidance, Raj continued his journey of self-discovery and spiritual growth. He knew that the gates to self-destructive hell would always be there, but armed with wisdom and practice, he had the power to navigate through them, choosing a path of light and liberation.

And so, the tale of Raj's encounter with the sage Devan became a timeless reminder that lust, anger, and greed are indeed the three gates to self-destructive hell. Yet, with self-awareness, discernment, and the guidance of wisdom, one can transcend their grasp and find the path to inner peace and freedom.

Seasons of Happiness and Distress

"*The nonpermanent appearance of happiness and distress, and their disappearance in due course, are like the appearance and disappearance of winter and summer seasons.*"

In a picturesque village, nestled amidst rolling hills, there lived a venerable old sage named Vasudev. His wisdom was as deep as the ocean, and people sought his counsel in times of joy and sorrow.

One day, a young traveler named Maya arrived at Vasudev's hermitage, seeking answers to the eternal questions of life. As they sat under the shade of a towering tree, Maya asked, "O wise sage, why do happiness and distress seem so fleeting? They come and go like the changing seasons. Is there a way to find lasting contentment?"

Vasudev smiled warmly and replied, "My dear traveler, just as the seasons of winter and summer appear and disappear in due course, so do happiness and distress in the journey of life. They are impermanent, like passing clouds in the sky."

Maya nodded thoughtfully, and Vasudev continued, "Understand that both happiness and distress are part of life's natural rhythm. Like the changing seasons, they come and go, guided by the cosmic dance of time. Embrace them with grace and equanimity."

"But how can one find lasting contentment amidst these ever-changing tides?" Maya inquired.

Vasudev's eyes twinkled with ancient wisdom as he shared a profound teaching. "The key lies in recognizing the impermanence of both happiness and distress," he said. "Neither remains forever. When you understand this truth, you no longer cling to moments of happiness or despair in the same way."

Maya listened intently, absorbing the sage's profound insights.

Vasudev continued, "Learn to appreciate the transient nature of experiences without attachment. Savor moments of happiness with gratitude, knowing they will eventually pass. And when distress clouds your horizon, remember that it too shall fade, making way for new opportunities and joys."

As the days turned into weeks, Maya spent time in the company of Vasudev, learning the art of embracing life's ever-changing seasons with equanimity.

One evening, as the sun painted the sky in hues of gold, Maya expressed her gratitude to the sage. "Your wisdom has brought me a new perspective on life," she said. "By understanding the impermanence of happiness and distress, I find greater peace and contentment within."

Vasudev smiled, his heart filled with joy. "May you continue to journey through life's seasons with grace and wisdom," he said. "Remember that every moment, whether joyful or challenging, is an opportunity for growth and learning."

As Maya bid farewell to the sage's hermitage, she carried the timeless teachings in her heart. She knew that life's seasons would continue to change, but she now had the wisdom to navigate them with an open heart and a serene mind.

And so, the tale of Maya's encounter with the sage Vasudev became a timeless reminder that the nonpermanent appearance of happiness and distress is akin to the changing seasons of winter and summer. Embrace life's moments with gratitude and grace, knowing that every experience is a fleeting part of the grand tapestry of existence. Through this understanding, one can find lasting contentment amidst the eternal dance of life.

Embracing the Law of Change

"*Change is the law of the universe. You can be a millionaire, or a pauper in an instant.*"

In a bustling city, where life's rhythm beat to the tune of opportunity and uncertainty, lived a man named Aryan. He was a hardworking and ambitious entrepreneur, always striving to build his empire and secure a prosperous future.

One day, as Aryan sat in his office overlooking the city's skyline, his trusted friend and mentor, Rohan, joined him for a conversation. Rohan was a wise and experienced businessman, who had weathered many storms in his own entrepreneurial journey.

"Aryan," Rohan said with a calm smile, "I see the fire of ambition burning bright within you. It's commendable to strive for success but remember that change is the law of the universe."

Curious, Aryan asked, "What do you mean, Rohan?"

Rohan replied, "Life is an ever-changing tapestry of circumstances. Just as the sun rises and sets, the tides ebb and flow, and the seasons transition, so does our journey through success and failure."

He continued, "You can be a millionaire, basking in the glory of success, and in an instant, circumstances can change, and you may face challenges that bring you to the brink of paucity."

Aryan listened intently, recognizing the truth in Rohan's words. He had seen many stories of success and downfall in the business world, but Rohan's perspective provided a deeper understanding.

"Does this mean I should fear change?" Aryan asked.

Rohan shook his head gently. "No, my dear friend," he said. "Embrace change as an inevitable part of life. Adaptability is the key to navigating the ebb and flow of circumstances. Stay grounded in your values, and let change be a catalyst for growth and resilience."

As weeks turned into months, Aryan continued to build his business empire, but this time with a new awareness of the law of change. He learned to cherish the successes without becoming complacent and faced challenges with a steadfast spirit.

One day, an unexpected economic downturn shook the business world, affecting Aryan's industry as well. Many businesses faced struggles, and Aryan's empire experienced a setback.

As he navigated through this challenging phase, Aryan remembered Rohan's wisdom. He remained resolute, making difficult decisions with a steady mind, and adapted his strategies to the changing landscape.

Months passed, and the tides began to turn. Aryan's resilience and adaptability bore fruit, and his business gradually regained its strength. He realized that the law of change had indeed been his greatest teacher, helping him grow as an entrepreneur and as an individual.

One evening, as the sun set over the city, Aryan met Rohan once again. "Your words were my guiding light," Aryan said with gratitude. "Change taught me the art of resilience and the value of embracing life's uncertainties."

Rohan smiled, his eyes reflecting the wisdom of a life well-lived. "Change is a constant companion on life's journey," he said. "By embracing its flow and being open to its lessons, we grow in strength and wisdom."

And so, the tale of Aryan's encounter with Rohan became a timeless reminder that change is the law of the universe. It can transform a millionaire into a pauper and vice versa. Yet, with resilience, adaptability, and an open heart, one can navigate the ever-changing tides and find success in the ebb and flow of life.

The Eternal Reward of Good Deeds

"*No one who does good work will ever come to a bad end, either here or in the world to come.*"

In a quaint village surrounded by lush forests and glistening rivers, there lived a humble and kind-hearted man named Samar. Known for his generosity and compassion, Samar was always ready to lend a helping hand to anyone in need.

One day, a traveler passing through the village approached Samar with a curious expression. "Samar," the traveler asked, "why do you tirelessly perform good deeds for others? What drives you to be so selfless?"

Samar smiled warmly and replied, "In the depths of my heart, I believe that no one who does good work will ever come to a bad end, either here or in the world to come. The universe rewards goodness with blessings, and the path of selflessness brings its own fulfillment."

The traveler marveled at Samar's unwavering faith and asked, "But how can you be so certain of this truth?"

Samar shared a tale that had been passed down through generations in his village.

Long ago, there lived a kind and diligent farmer named Arjun. Despite facing many challenges, Arjun remained steadfast in his good deeds. He generously shared his harvest with those in need, regardless of his own hardships.

One year, a severe drought struck the region, and many farmers suffered devastating losses. Yet, Arjun's crops miraculously thrived. People marveled at his fortune and wondered if the heavens had favored him.

One evening, as the sun painted the sky with hues of gold, the village gathered around a bonfire. An elder shared a revelation he had received in his dreams.

In his dream, the village's guardian deity appeared and spoke, "Arjun's good deeds have touched the heart of the heavens. The universe has recognized his selflessness and showered him with blessings. No one who does good work will ever come to a bad end, either here or in the world to come."

The village was filled with awe and gratitude, understanding that goodness begets goodness and that the universe rewards those who sow seeds of compassion and selflessness.

As the traveler listened to Samar's tale, his heart overflowed with inspiration. He had witnessed firsthand the impact of Samar's kindness on the villagers' lives and understood the wisdom behind his beliefs.

With newfound faith, the traveler embarked on his journey, carrying the wisdom of Samar's words with him.

In the years that followed, Samar's selfless acts continued to sow seeds of compassion in the hearts of many. His village prospered, not only in material abundance but also in the richness of human connections.

One day, as the traveler returned to the village, he found Samar sitting under a banyan tree, his face radiant with contentment.

"Your words have become my guiding light," the traveler said to Samar. "I have witnessed the truth of your beliefs in my own journey. Goodness begets goodness, and the universe rewards those who perform good deeds."

Samar nodded, his eyes reflecting the wisdom of a life well-lived. "In the cycle of giving and receiving, goodness prevails," he said. "May the world be blessed with more hearts like yours, spreading love and compassion to every corner."

And so, the tale of Samar and the traveler became a timeless reminder that no one who does good work will ever come to a bad end, either here or in the world to come. The universe embraces those who selflessly contribute to the welfare of others, blessing them with the eternal reward of fulfillment and abundant goodness.

The Wisdom of Detachment

"*T****he awakened sages call a person wise when all their undertakings are free from anxiety about results."***

In the tranquil abode of an ancient forest, a renowned sage named Yogi Dharmanand lived in harmony with nature. Seekers from far and wide sought his wisdom, drawn by tales of his profound insights.

One day, a young scholar named Tara ventured into the forest, seeking answers to life's perplexing questions. She found Yogi Dharmanand seated under a majestic tree, exuding an aura of serenity.

"O revered sage," Tara said with humility, "how does one attain true wisdom?"

Yogi Dharmanand smiled gently and replied, "The awakened sages call a person wise when all their undertakings are free from anxiety about results."

Curious, Tara inquired, "But isn't it natural to desire positive outcomes for our efforts?"

The sage's eyes sparkled with ancient wisdom as he shared a parable with Tara.

"In a nearby village," Yogi Dharmanand began, "there lived a skilled sculptor named Siddharth. His passion for carving exquisite sculptures was unparalleled. People came from distant lands to commission his work, expecting nothing but perfection."

"One day, a weary traveler approached Siddharth with a block of marble. 'Create a statue that will bring me great fame and wealth,' the traveler demanded."

"Siddharth accepted the task but, instead of focusing on fame and wealth, he immersed himself fully in the process of creation. He carved with love, pouring his heart into each stroke of the chisel, without attachment to the outcome."

"As the days turned into weeks, the statue gradually took shape. Its beauty was beyond words, capturing the essence of divinity and grace."

"When the traveler returned to claim his statue, he was awestruck by its magnificence. He offered Siddharth a fortune in exchange, but the sculptor declined, saying, 'My satisfaction lies in the act of creation itself. The result is not mine to claim.'"

Tara pondered the parable, recognizing the profound message within.

Yogi Dharmanand continued, "True wisdom lies in offering our best efforts to the world, free from the burden of attachment to the results. When we act with pure intentions and surrender to the flow of life, we attain a state of inner peace and clarity."

"As you undertake your endeavors, focus on the present moment, cherishing the process rather than being consumed by the outcomes. Detach yourself from expectations and trust that the universe will unfold its plan in its own divine time."

Tara felt a sense of liberation wash over her, as if a weight had been lifted from her shoulders. She thanked Yogi Dharmanand for his wisdom and vowed to practice detachment in her life's pursuits.

In the days that followed, Tara absorbed Yogi Dharmanand's teachings, immersing herself in the journey rather than obsessing over destinations. She found solace in the art of living in the present, unburdened by anxieties about the future.

As she bid farewell to the sage and journeyed back to the outside world, Tara knew that she had received a priceless gift—the wisdom of detachment.

And so, the tale of Tara's encounter with Yogi Dharmanand became a timeless reminder that the awakened sages call a person wise when all their undertakings are free from anxiety about results. In the realm of true wisdom, one finds peace and contentment by embracing the present moment, allowing life's river to flow freely, and surrendering to the divine currents that guide us all.

The Battle Within

"A *person is his own friend as well as his own enemy.*"
In a bustling city, where the streets were alive with the hustle and bustle of daily life, lived a man named Arjun. He was known for his intelligence and charm, but behind his cheerful exterior lay an inner struggle that few could perceive.

One evening, as the sun dipped below the horizon, Arjun sought solace in the company of an elderly philosopher named Guruji. The wise Guruji was renowned for his ability to unravel the mysteries of the human mind.

"Master," Arjun said with a troubled expression, "I find myself caught in a perpetual conflict within my own being. There are times when I am my best friend, supporting and uplifting myself, and yet, in other moments, I become my own worst enemy, undermining my confidence and self-worth."

Guruji nodded, understanding the internal strife that Arjun described. "My dear child," he said, "the battle between being one's friend and enemy is an eternal struggle that resides within every soul. It is a reflection of the duality that exists in human experience."

Arjun looked intrigued, urging Guruji to shed light on this inner conflict.

Guruji continued, "You see, every person carries within them two forces—the higher self and the lower self. The higher self represents the divine essence, the spark of wisdom and compassion that seeks growth and self-improvement."

"The lower self, on the other hand, is driven by ego, fear, and desires. It can lead you astray and cloud your judgment, making you your own enemy."

Arjun reflected on Guruji's words, realizing that he had indeed experienced both aspects within himself.

Guruji continued, "To find balance and peace within, one must learn to cultivate the higher self while taming the lower self. Embrace self-awareness and self-compassion, for they will help you discern between thoughts and actions that uplift and those that bring discord."

He added, "Treat yourself as you would a dear friend. Encourage yourself during moments of doubt, celebrate your successes, and be patient with your imperfections. At the same time, be vigilant and gentle when the lower self-attempts to derail your journey."

As the weeks passed, Arjun practiced Guruji's teachings with dedication. He learned to recognize the patterns of his higher and lower self, embracing the former and gently steering the latter toward positive transformation.

One day, Arjun returned to Guruji with a smile of newfound clarity. "Master," he said, "I am beginning to understand the dance between being my own friend and enemy. By nurturing my higher self and being compassionate towards the lower self, I find greater peace within."

Guruji smiled, knowing that Arjun had taken an important step on the path of self-awareness and growth.

As the years passed, Arjun continued to embrace the dual aspects within him—the friend and the enemy. He discovered that the key to inner harmony lay in nurturing his higher self, thus weakening the power of the lower self's negativity.

And so, the tale of Arjun's encounter with Guruji became a timeless reminder that a person is indeed their own friend as well as their own enemy. By cultivating self-awareness, compassion, and the strength to choose the path of growth, one can overcome inner conflict and find the inner peace that resides at the core of every soul.

Embracing the Path of Purpose

"**A** person's own duty, even if imperfectly performed, is better than doing another person's duty well."

In a vibrant village, where the air was filled with the aroma of blooming flowers, lived a diligent young woman named Maya. She was known for her unwavering dedication to her work and her relentless pursuit of perfection.

One day, Maya's neighbor, Ravi, a skilled artisan, approached her with a request. "Maya," he said, "I have fallen ill, and I have a few unfinished art pieces that need attention. Could you lend your expertise and complete them for me?"

Maya hesitated, torn between her desire to help and her reluctance to deviate from her own work. She was a skilled weaver, and her loom was filled with intricate patterns waiting to be woven into tapestries of beauty.

Ravi noticed Maya's inner struggle and gently said, "I understand your dilemma, Maya. But consider this: a person's own duty, even if imperfectly performed, is better than doing another person's duty well."

These words struck a chord within Maya, making her reflect on the meaning behind them.

Later that evening, Maya visited Ravi and offered her assistance with his art pieces. As she carefully worked on the intricate carvings, she found a sense of fulfillment in her act of kindness.

Weeks passed, and Ravi recovered, grateful for Maya's support during his challenging time. As a gesture of gratitude, Ravi gifted Maya one of his finished artworks—a magnificent sculpture that embodied the essence of gratitude and interdependence.

As Maya placed the sculpture in her home, she realized the profound truth behind Ravi's words. Each person has a unique path and a calling—a duty that is uniquely their own. Embracing one's duty, even if imperfectly performed, allows the individual to experience a sense of purpose and fulfillment.

With newfound clarity, Maya returned to her loom with renewed passion. Instead of chasing perfection, she wove each tapestry with love and dedication, knowing that her duty as a weaver was her path to contentment.

Over time, Maya's tapestries gained renown in the village for their unique charm and authenticity. People were drawn to her work, not only for its beauty but also for the passion that flowed through each thread.

One day, a visitor asked Maya, "What is the secret behind the enchanting allure of your tapestries?"

Maya smiled and replied, "The secret lies in embracing my own duty with love and dedication. Each thread woven with purpose becomes a part of me, and that essence finds its way into the fabric of my creations."

As word of Maya's wisdom and artistry spread, she became an inspiration to many in the village. Her journey taught them the importance of finding purpose in their own duties, rather than comparing themselves to others.

And so, the tale of Maya's encounter with Ravi became a timeless reminder that a person's own duty, even if imperfectly performed, is better than doing another person's duty well. Embrace your path with authenticity, for therein lies the key to contentment and the discovery of your true calling in the tapestry of life.

The Serenity of the Mind

"One who has control over the mind is tranquil in heat and cold, in pleasure and pain, and in honor and dishonor."

In a remote mountainous region, where the air was crisp and the beauty of nature untamed, there lived a wise monk named Swami Devananda. He was revered for his profound understanding of the human mind and his unshakable tranquility in all circumstances.

One day, a curious young traveler named Kavya arrived at the doorstep of Swami Devananda's humble ashram. Intrigued by the tales of the monk's serenity, she sought his guidance to find inner peace amidst life's challenges.

Swami Devananda welcomed Kavya with a warm smile and invited her to sit beside him. "My child," he said, "inner peace lies in having control over the mind."

Kavya was eager to learn more and asked, "But how does one attain such control, revered Swami?"

The monk's eyes sparkled with profound wisdom as he shared a tale that had been passed down through generations.

"In a bustling city, there lived a young merchant named Raghav," Swami Devananda began. "Raghav was ambitious and hardworking, but he found himself tossed between waves of joy and despair as he navigated life's challenges."

"One day, Raghav heard of a sage who was said to possess the secret to mastering the mind. Determined to find peace, he embarked on a long journey to meet the sage."

"After days of arduous travel, Raghav finally reached the sage's abode. With humility, he asked, 'O revered sage, how can I gain control over my mind and find tranquility amidst the storms of life?'"

"The sage looked into Raghav's eyes and replied, 'Control your mind, and you shall find tranquility in all circumstances. The mind is like a wild horse, difficult to tame, but with patience and practice, it can be brought under control.'"

"Inspired by the sage's words, Raghav decided to stay in the ashram and learn the art of controlling the mind."

With curiosity, Kavya asked, "Did Raghav succeed in taming his mind, revered Swami?"

Swami Devananda smiled and continued, "Indeed, my child. Raghav immersed himself in meditation and mindfulness, observing the fluctuations of his thoughts without judgment."

"With each passing day, he became more aware of his mind's tendencies and learned to redirect its energy towards positive and uplifting thoughts. He embraced the present moment, letting go of regrets from the past and anxieties about the future."

"As Raghav's mind became tranquil, he found inner peace that transcended the external circumstances of life. The sweltering heat of summer no longer bothered him, and the freezing cold of winter failed to disturb his equanimity. Pleasure and pain became passing sensations, and honor and dishonor ceased to sway his self-worth."

Kavya was fascinated by the tale and asked, "How can I too attain such control over my mind, revered Swami?"

Swami Devananda's eyes held a gentle light as he said, "The journey to master the mind begins with self-awareness and the willingness to practice regularly. Engage in mindfulness, meditation, and self-reflection. Cultivate virtues like patience, compassion, and gratitude."

"Through these practices, you will discover that the key to serenity lies within you. The mind is like a vast ocean, and its waves can be stilled by the power of your inner presence."

Over the course of her stay, Kavya soaked in Swami Devananda's teachings, dedicating herself to the pursuit of inner peace. She realized that by gaining control over her mind, she could indeed become tranquil in all circumstances.

And so, the tale of Kavya's encounter with Swami Devananda became
a timeless reminder that one who has control over the mind is tranquil in
heat and cold, in pleasure and pain, and in honor and dishonor. Through the
practice of mindfulness and self-awareness, one can unlock the door to inner
peace and find serenity amidst the ever-changing tides of life.

Liberation from the Chains of Desire

"Those who are motivated only by desire for the fruits of action are miserable, for they are constantly anxious about the results of what they do."

In a bustling town, where dreams and ambitions thrived, lived a young man named Arjun. He was talented and hardworking, driven by a burning desire to achieve success and recognition in his chosen field.

One day, Arjun's father, a wise and experienced businessman, noticed a restlessness in his son's eyes. Sensing the turmoil within him, he invited Arjun for a conversation under the shade of a blooming tree in their garden.

"Arjun, my son," his father said with a gentle smile, "I have noticed that you are constantly anxious about the results of your actions. Your desires seem to consume you, making you miserable even amidst your accomplishments."

Arjun sighed, feeling a weight lift off his chest at his father's perceptive words. "You are right, Father," he confessed. "I feel a constant need to prove myself and achieve more. Yet, the fruits of my actions never seem to be enough to quench this insatiable thirst."

His father nodded with understanding and shared a tale from his own youth—a story that had been passed down by generations.

"In a distant kingdom, there lived a young warrior named Veer. He was fiercely skilled in combat and determined to earn recognition and rewards from the king. Veer believed that his worth as a warrior depended solely on the fruits of his battles."

"One day, a wise sage named Siddharth crossed paths with Veer. The sage noticed the fire of desire burning in Veer's eyes and sensed his internal struggle. He approached Veer and offered him counsel."

"'Young warrior,' Siddharth said, 'desire for the fruits of action is a chain that binds the soul. It makes one endlessly chase fleeting mirages of success and accolades, leading to perpetual misery.'"

"Veer was taken aback by the sage's words. He had always believed that his desires fueled his determination."

Siddharth continued, "'Desire can indeed fuel determination, but when it becomes the sole motivation, it creates a cycle of suffering. Instead, focus on performing your duties with excellence, dedicating your actions to a higher purpose, without attachment to the results.'"

"As Veer pondered the sage's wisdom, he realized that the pursuit of recognition and rewards had indeed brought him anxiety and discontent. He decided to adopt Siddharth's counsel and changed his approach to battle."

"In time, Veer found a new sense of freedom in dedicating his actions to a higher cause. He fought with courage and skill, not for personal gain, but to protect the innocent and uphold justice."

Arjun listened intently to his father's tale, feeling a shift within himself.

His father continued, "My son, understand that life's journey is not just about achieving goals but about finding purpose and meaning in every action. When you detach yourself from the desire for specific outcomes, you will discover a sense of peace and fulfillment in the process itself."

Arjun felt a newfound clarity as he realized that his father's words held the key to liberation from the chains of desire. He embraced the wisdom and vowed to dedicate himself to his work without attachment to the fruits of his actions.

Over time, Arjun found a profound sense of contentment and joy in his pursuits. He no longer measured his worth solely by external accomplishments but derived satisfaction from the passion and dedication he poured into his work.

And so, the tale of Arjun's conversation with his father became a timeless reminder that those who are motivated only by desire for the fruits of action are indeed miserable, for they are constantly anxious about the results of what they do. True liberation lies in dedicating one's actions to a higher purpose and finding fulfillment in the journey itself, detached from the outcomes that are beyond our control.

The Serenity of Self-Realization

"T_he soul who meditates on the Self is content to serve the Self and rests satisfied within the Self."_

In a peaceful hermitage tucked away amidst verdant forests, lived a serene sage named Aarav. His eyes radiated wisdom, and his heart was filled with boundless compassion for all beings.

One day, a curious traveler named Meera arrived at Aarav's hermitage, seeking answers to life's profound questions. Intrigued by the sage's tranquil demeanor, Meera asked, "O venerable sage, how does one find true contentment and peace within?"

Aarav smiled gently and replied, "The path to contentment lies in meditating on the Self—the essence that resides within each being. When one realizes the divinity within, they find contentment in serving the Self and rest satisfied within the Self."

Meera was intrigued and sought to understand this concept more deeply. "But what does it mean to meditate on the Self?" she inquired.

Aarav gestured to the natural beauty surrounding them—the rustling leaves, the glistening stream, and the majestic mountains. "In this vast creation, the same life force flows through all living beings," he explained. "Meditating on the Self means recognizing this interconnectedness and seeking the divine essence that permeates every soul."

He continued, "By turning inward through contemplation and mindfulness, one can shed the layers of ego and desire, unveiling the pure and radiant Self that is untouched by external circumstances."

Intrigued by Aarav's wisdom, Meera decided to spend time in the hermitage, seeking to learn the art of self-meditation.

In the following weeks, Meera immersed herself in meditation and introspection. Under Aarav's guidance, she learned to quiet the noise of the world and explore the depths of her own consciousness.

As days turned into weeks, Meera experienced moments of profound clarity. She glimpsed the vast interconnectedness of all life and felt a sense of contentment that transcended fleeting desires.

One evening, as the setting sun painted the sky in hues of gold, Meera shared her experience with Aarav. "I have begun to touch the essence of the Self within," she said, her eyes shining with newfound understanding. "I feel a deep sense of contentment and peace, as if I have come home to myself."

Aarav nodded; his heart filled with joy. "The Self is the eternal abode of serenity," he said. "When you recognize your connection to the divine within, you rest satisfied in the tranquil embrace of your true nature."

Over time, Meera continued her journey of self-meditation. She discovered that contentment arose not from external achievements or possessions, but from the realization of her inherent divinity.

As she bid farewell to Aarav's hermitage and embarked on her onward journey, Meera carried the wisdom of self-meditation in her heart. She knew that the path to lasting contentment lay in recognizing the Self within and serving that divine essence with love and compassion.

And so, the tale of Meera's encounter with Sage Aarav became a timeless reminder that the soul who meditates on the Self is indeed content to serve the Self and rests satisfied within the Self. Through self-realization and inner contemplation, one discovers the boundless peace that lies within, connecting them to the infinite source of contentment and fulfillment.

The Unwavering Flame

"When meditation is mastered, the mind is unwavering like the flame of a lamp in a windless place."

In the heart of a serene mountain range, where the air was crisp and the tranquility palpable, there resided a venerable monk named Master Aditya. His eyes glowed with the light of inner peace, and his presence exuded a sense of profound stillness.

One day, a curious traveler named Rajiv arrived at the monastery, seeking guidance on the path to inner calm. Rajiv had heard tales of Master Aditya's mastery in meditation and his ability to maintain a steady mind amidst life's storms.

Approaching the revered monk, Rajiv asked, "O Master, how can I find such unwavering stillness in the mind?"

Master Aditya smiled warmly and beckoned Rajiv to sit beside him. "The key to unwavering stillness lies in the practice of meditation," he said. "When meditation is mastered, the mind becomes steady, like the flame of a lamp in a windless place."

Intrigued, Rajiv inquired, "But how can one master meditation?"

Master Aditya's eyes glimmered with the wisdom of ages as he shared a tale of ancient times—a story that had been passed down from one generation of monks to another.

"In a distant kingdom, there lived a young scholar named Arnav. He was gifted with intellect but carried a restless mind, always swayed by the winds of desire and worry."

"One day, a wise sage named Yogi Rishi came to the kingdom, renowned for his mastery in meditation. People flocked to him, seeking the key to tranquility."

"Arnav, intrigued by the tales of Yogi Rishi's serene presence, approached him and asked, 'O revered sage, how can I find peace in my restless mind?'"

"Yogi Rishi smiled and said, 'Meditation is the path to mastering the mind. Just as a flame remains unwavering in a windless place, so does the mind remain steady when trained through meditation.'"

"Intrigued by the sage's words, Arnav sought Yogi Rishi's guidance and began his meditation journey. Day after day, he dedicated himself to the practice, observing the thoughts that arose and learning to let them pass like clouds in the sky."

"As weeks turned into months, Arnav noticed a subtle change within himself. The winds of desires and worries no longer tossed his mind as violently. Instead, it became like a serene lake, reflecting the world with clarity."

Rajiv was captivated by the tale and asked, "Did Arnav find the unwavering stillness he sought, revered Master?"

Master Aditya nodded and replied, "Indeed, through persistent practice, Arnav's meditation bore fruit. He discovered the power of the present moment—the anchor of unwavering stillness."

"He realized that the mind's fluctuations are like passing clouds, and the soul's essence is the eternal sky. By connecting with that essence through meditation, he found the unwavering flame of inner peace."

Inspired by Master Aditya's words, Rajiv decided to immerse himself in the practice of meditation. He vowed to learn the art of stillness and to embrace each moment with unwavering presence.

In the days that followed, Rajiv meditated diligently, nurturing the flame of inner peace within him. He began to experience moments of profound clarity and tranquility, sensing the unwavering nature of his mind when centered in the present moment.

As Rajiv continued his journey, he realized that the practice of meditation was not a destination but a lifelong path. It was a journey of discovering the boundless serenity that resides within, like the flame of a lamp in a windless place.

And so, the tale of Rajiv's encounter with Master Aditya became a timeless reminder that when meditation is mastered, the mind indeed becomes unwavering like the flame of a lamp in a windless place. Through dedicated practice, one discovers the stillness and serenity that lie at the core of their being, illuminating the path to inner peace amidst life's ever-changing currents.

The Path to Steady Wisdom

"*A person can achieve steady wisdom when they renounce all desires for sense gratification.*"

In a quaint village nestled amidst rolling hills, lived a sage named Swami Amar. His eyes sparkled with the wisdom of ages, and his presence exuded an aura of tranquility.

One day, a curious villager named Anika sought Swami Amar's guidance. She had heard stories of his profound wisdom and sought to understand the secrets to inner peace and steady wisdom.

Approaching the sage with humility, Anika said, "O revered Swami, I am often tormented by my desires for sense gratification. How can I attain steady wisdom and find lasting contentment?"

Swami Amar smiled gently and beckoned Anika to sit beside him. "The path to steady wisdom lies in renouncing desires for sense gratification," he said. "When one lets go of attachment to fleeting pleasures, the mind becomes clear, and wisdom finds its abode."

Intrigued, Anika asked, "But how can one renounce desires when they seem so powerful and tempting?"

Swami Amar's eyes glowed with compassion as he shared a tale—a timeless story that had been passed down through generations.

"In a bustling kingdom, there lived a wealthy merchant named Ravi. He possessed abundant riches and indulged in every material pleasure life had to offer. Yet, despite his possessions, he felt a void within—a persistent restlessness that could not be quenched."

"One day, Ravi heard of a wise sage named Muni who had renounced the world to seek inner truth. Intrigued, he sought Muni's guidance, hoping to find the peace he so desperately yearned for."

"Upon meeting Muni, Ravi expressed his discontent and asked, 'O venerable sage, how can I find inner peace and steady wisdom?'"

"Muni smiled serenely and said, 'Steady wisdom can be attained when you renounce desires for sense gratification. The material world may offer temporary pleasures, but true contentment lies beyond its fleeting allure.'"

"Intrigued, Ravi asked, 'But how can I let go of desires that seem to have a tight grip on my heart?'"

"Muni replied, 'Reflect on the impermanence of material pleasures. Realize that they offer momentary happiness, but they are like passing clouds in the vast sky of life.'"

"Ravi listened intently to Muni's words and decided to embark on a journey of self-discovery. He practiced detachment, letting go of his attachment to material possessions and transient pleasures."

"In time, Ravi began to experience a newfound sense of freedom. As he released the chains of desire, his mind became clear, and wisdom began to dawn within him."

Anika listened with rapt attention, understanding the profound message within the tale.

Swami Amar continued, "True wisdom arises when one sees the impermanence of the world and seeks lasting contentment within. By renouncing desires for sense gratification, the mind becomes steady, like a tranquil lake reflecting the truth of existence."

Inspired by Swami Amar's wisdom, Anika vowed to walk the path of renunciation and seek steady wisdom. She understood that by detaching herself from the ephemeral desires of the world, she could find the eternal peace that resided within her heart.

In the days that followed, Anika practiced mindfulness and detachment, seeking to cultivate wisdom and inner contentment. Gradually, she felt a newfound clarity and serenity, knowing that she was on the path to steady wisdom.

And so, the tale of Anika's encounter with Swami Amar became a timeless reminder that a person can indeed achieve steady wisdom when they renounce all desires for sense gratification. By embracing the path of inner contentment, one finds true liberation from the ever-changing tides of desires, discovering the eternal wisdom that resides within their soul.

The Dual Nature of the Mind

"*A person should elevate themselves by their mind, and not degrade themselves. The mind is their friend, and also their enemy.*"

In a vibrant city, where ambitions soared and dreams took flight, lived a young individual named Aanya. She possessed a curious mind and an indomitable spirit, eager to make her mark in the world.

One evening, as the sun dipped below the horizon, Aanya found herself deep in contemplation at a serene park. The whispers of the wind and the rustling leaves seemed to echo the questions in her heart.

Lost in her thoughts, Aanya's gaze fell upon an elderly woman who sat nearby, radiating an aura of wisdom and grace. Intrigued, she approached the woman and asked, "Ma'am, can you share the secret to self-elevation and inner strength?"

The elderly woman smiled warmly and replied, "My dear, the secret lies within your mind. Elevate yourself by your thoughts, and you shall soar to great heights. But be wary, for the same mind can also become your worst enemy if not directed with wisdom."

Intrigued, Aanya asked, "How can I harness the power of my mind, and why is it both my friend and enemy?"

The wise woman shared a tale that had been passed down through generations—a story that carried timeless lessons.

"In a bustling kingdom, there lived a young prince named Arjun. He was well-versed in the arts, brave in battles, and compassionate toward his subjects. But beneath his confident exterior lay a constant battle within his mind."

"Arjun's mind was like a battlefield, where thoughts of doubt, fear, and ego waged war against his virtues. One moment, it propelled him to greatness, and the next, it held him captive in self-doubt."

"One day, a revered sage named Guruji visited the kingdom. Sensing Arjun's inner struggle, he approached the young prince and said, 'O noble soul, the mind is the key to self-elevation. Elevate yourself by cultivating thoughts of courage, compassion, and wisdom.'"

"'But beware,' Guruji warned, 'for the same mind can also degrade you if consumed by negativity, envy, and greed. It can become a formidable enemy, imprisoning you in a cycle of suffering.'"

Arjun listened intently to Guruji's words, recognizing the truth within them. Determined to master his mind, he sought Guruji's guidance in the practice of mindfulness and self-awareness.

As weeks turned into months, Arjun learned to observe the fluctuations of his mind without judgment. He chose to elevate himself by nurturing positive thoughts and virtues, while gently releasing those that brought him down.

Gradually, Arjun's mind became his ally, guiding him toward wise decisions and fostering inner strength. He found that by harnessing the power of his thoughts, he could achieve greatness and uplift those around him.

Aanya listened to the tale with fascination, recognizing the relevance to her own journey. "But how can I master my mind and elevate myself?" she asked.

The wise woman replied, "Cultivate mindfulness through meditation and self-reflection. Choose thoughts that empower you and others. Let go of negativity and self-limiting beliefs. Remember that your mind is both your friend and enemy—nurture it like a garden, and it will bloom with wisdom and strength."

Inspired by the woman's guidance, Aanya embarked on a journey of self-discovery, determined to elevate herself through her thoughts and choices. She understood that the mind held the key to her growth and that by taming its wild nature, she could unlock the vast potential within her soul.

And so, the tale of Aanya's encounter with the wise woman became a timeless reminder that a person should indeed elevate themselves by their mind and not degrade themselves. The mind is a powerful force, capable of both empowering and imprisoning us. Through mindfulness and self-awareness, we can transform our mind into a loyal friend, guiding us to greatness and inner strength on the journey of life.

The Power of Purposeful Action

"*Perform your obligatory duty, because action is indeed better than inaction.*" In a bustling city, where life moved at a frantic pace, lived a diligent young professional named Rohan. He was skilled in his work and dedicated to excelling in his career.

One day, amidst the chaos of deadlines and responsibilities, Rohan found himself overwhelmed by the weight of his obligations. Seeking solace, he visited his wise grandfather, a man known for his profound insights on life.

As Rohan poured out his anxieties, his grandfather listened attentively and offered a reassuring smile. "My dear Rohan," he said, "remember that life's journey is filled with duties and responsibilities. Embrace your obligatory duty and perform it with dedication."

Curious, Rohan asked, "But why should I continue to act when it feels like the weight of the world is upon me? Wouldn't it be better to escape into inaction?"

His grandfather gently replied, "Performing your duty is a testament to your strength and determination. Inaction may provide temporary respite, but it will not lead to growth and fulfillment. Action, my boy, is indeed better than inaction."

Intrigued by his grandfather's wisdom, Rohan sought to understand the essence of purposeful action. His grandfather shared a tale—a story that held timeless truths.

"In a serene village, there lived a compassionate farmer named Alok. He tilled the soil with dedication, knowing that his labor would nourish the community. Alok was content with his life and found joy in his simple yet meaningful duties."

"One day, a wandering monk named Swami Vishal arrived in the village. Sensing a deep wisdom in the monk's eyes, the villagers gathered to seek his counsel."

"Alok, too, was drawn to the presence of Swami Vishal and asked, 'O revered Swami, how can one find fulfillment amidst the burdens of daily life?'"

"Swami Vishal smiled and replied, 'Perform your obligatory duty with a heart full of love and dedication. Embrace each task as an offering to the greater good, knowing that your actions, no matter how small, have the potential to create ripples of positive impact.'"

"'Find purpose in your actions,' the Swami continued. 'Let them be driven by compassion and a desire to contribute to the welfare of others. In doing so, you will discover the true meaning of fulfillment.'"

As Rohan listened to the tale, a sense of clarity washed over him. He understood that his sense of burden stemmed from losing sight of the purpose behind his actions.

With newfound determination, Rohan returned to his work, embracing each task as an opportunity to contribute and make a difference. He understood that purposeful action was the key to finding fulfillment amidst life's challenges.

Over time, Rohan's efforts bore fruit, and he found a sense of contentment and accomplishment in his work. He realized that even small actions, when performed with dedication and purpose, could have a profound impact on his life and the lives of those around him.

And so, the tale of Rohan's encounter with his wise grandfather became a timeless reminder that performing one's obligatory duty is indeed better than inaction. Purposeful action, driven by compassion and dedication, leads to growth, fulfillment, and a life that leaves a positive mark on the world.

The Seasons of Life

"*The nonpermanent appearance of happiness and distress, and their disappearance in due course, are like the appearance and disappearance of winter and summer seasons.*"

In a quaint village nestled between lush hills, lived a wise elder named Guruji. His words were like pearls of wisdom, cherished by all who sought his counsel.

One bright morning, a young villager named Rina approached Guruji with a heavy heart. "O wise Guruji," she said, "I am caught in the cycle of happiness and distress. How can I find lasting peace?"

Guruji smiled warmly and motioned for Rina to sit beside him. "Dear child, life is like the changing seasons—filled with the fleeting appearances of happiness and distress. Just as winter and summer come and go, so do life's joys and sorrows. They are impermanent, and their disappearance is inevitable."

Intrigued, Rina asked, "But how can I find lasting peace amidst this ever-changing cycle?"

Guruji shared a tale—a story passed down through generations—a tale that carried the wisdom of life's ebb and flow.

"In a distant kingdom, there lived a kind-hearted farmer named Dev. He toiled in the fields, sowing seeds in spring and reaping the harvest in autumn. Through the seasons, he remained equanimous, neither overly elated in times of abundance nor overly disheartened during periods of scarcity."

"One day, a wise wanderer named Yogi Tara visited the village. Intrigued by Dev's serene demeanor, she approached him and asked, 'O noble farmer, how do you find such tranquility amidst life's ever-changing fortunes?'"

"Dev smiled humbly and replied, 'The seasons of life taught me a valuable lesson. Just as the changing seasons are a natural rhythm of existence, so are the cycles of happiness and distress in life. I embrace both with gratitude, knowing that they are fleeting and will pass in due course.'"

"'When the sun shines, I rejoice in the abundance it brings. And when the storms rage, I hold steadfast, knowing that after every storm, the sun will shine again.'"

Yogi Tara listened with admiration, recognizing the profound wisdom in Dev's words.

Guruji continued, "Dear Rina, finding lasting peace lies in embracing life's impermanence. Neither happiness nor distress is permanent—they are mere visitors passing through the landscape of your journey."

"By cultivating a heart of acceptance and gratitude, you can navigate life's seasons with grace and equanimity. Embrace the happiness that comes your way and learn from the lessons in distress. Just as the seasons change, so does life, and in every moment, you have the power to choose your response."

Rina pondered Guruji's words, feeling a newfound sense of peace within. She understood that by embracing life's impermanence, she could find contentment in the present moment.

In the days that followed, Rina practiced Guruji's teachings, learning to navigate life's joys and sorrows with grace. She found solace in knowing that just as winter and summer seasons come and go, happiness and distress too will pass, making way for new experiences.

And so, the tale of Rina's encounter with Guruji became a timeless reminder that the nonpermanent appearance of happiness and distress, and their disappearance in due course, are indeed like the appearance and disappearance of winter and summer seasons. Embrace life's impermanence with gratitude and equanimity, for it is in the acceptance of change that true peace and contentment are found.

Embracing the Winds of Change

"Change is the law of the universe. You can be a millionaire, or a pauper in an instant."

In a bustling city, where dreams and aspirations intertwined, lived a young entrepreneur named Aiden. He was ambitious, driven by the desire to achieve great success and financial abundance.

One day, as Aiden was strolling through the vibrant streets, he noticed an old beggar sitting by the roadside. The beggar's eyes held a certain serenity that intrigued Aiden. Curiosity got the better of him, and he approached the old man.

"Sir, forgive my intrusion, but you seem content despite your humble circumstances," Aiden said respectfully. "How can you find peace amidst life's uncertainties?"

The old beggar smiled, his eyes reflecting a deep well of wisdom. "Ah, young one," he replied, "change is the law of the universe. In the blink of an eye, fortunes can shift—leaving you as a millionaire or a pauper."

Perplexed, Aiden asked, "But how can one find stability and security in such a world of constant flux?"

The beggar shared a tale—a story that had been passed down through generations—a tale that held the truth of life's ever-changing nature.

"In a prosperous kingdom, there lived a successful merchant named Keshav. He possessed great wealth and lived a life of abundance, basking in the glory of his riches. But deep within, he knew that the tides of fate could turn at any moment."

"One day, a wise sage named Siddharth came to the kingdom. Sensing Keshav's restlessness, he approached the merchant and said, 'O noble soul, change is the very fabric of existence. Embrace it with acceptance, for it is beyond your control.'"

"Keshav was intrigued and asked, 'But how can I find stability when everything around me is subject to change?'"

"Siddharth smiled and replied, 'Find stability within yourself—the unchanging core of your being. Just as the vast ocean remains calm at its depths despite the turbulent waves on its surface, so can you find tranquility within, amidst life's fluctuations.'"

The beggar paused for a moment before continuing, "Dear Aiden, realize that true stability comes from cultivating inner peace, not from external possessions or circumstances. By embracing change with equanimity, you free yourself from the shackles of attachment and fear."

As the old beggar spoke, Aiden felt a sense of revelation washing over him. He understood that life's uncertainties were an inherent part of the journey, and resisting change only led to suffering.

With newfound clarity, Aiden thanked the beggar for his profound insight and bid him farewell.

In the days that followed, Aiden reflected on the wisdom he had received. He began to embrace change with open arms, understanding that it was the very essence of life's journey. With a newfound focus on inner peace and acceptance, he found a sense of stability that transcended external circumstances.

And so, the tale of Aiden's encounter with the old beggar became a timeless reminder that change is indeed the law of the universe. Whether one becomes a millionaire, or a pauper is beyond their control. Embrace life's uncertainties with equanimity and find stability within the unchanging core of your being. It is in the acceptance of change that true peace and contentment are found amidst life's ever-shifting winds.

The Ocean of Inner Peace

"One who is not disturbed by the incessant flow of desires—that enter like rivers into the ocean, which is ever being filled but is always still—can alone achieve peace, and not the person who strives to satisfy such desires."

In a serene coastal village, where the gentle waves caressed the shore, lived a wise sage named Rishi. His tranquil presence and radiant smile attracted seekers from far and wide.

One sunny morning, a curious traveler named Maya arrived at Rishi's humble abode. She sought guidance on finding lasting peace amidst the chaos of life.

Approaching the sage with reverence, Maya asked, "O revered Rishi, my heart feels restless, pulled by endless desires. How can I find peace when the world bombards me with temptations?"

Rishi's eyes held the depth of ancient wisdom as he replied, "Dear one, desires are like rivers that flow into the ocean of your consciousness. The ocean remains calm and still, regardless of the rivers that pour into it. Similarly, inner peace arises when you remain undisturbed by the incessant flow of desires."

Intrigued, Maya inquired, "But how can I attain such tranquility when desires seem so overwhelming?"

Rishi shared a tale—a story rooted in timeless truths—a tale that would offer Maya profound insights.

"In a bustling town, there lived a prosperous merchant named Amar. Despite his vast wealth, Amar felt a void within, constantly seeking to satisfy his insatiable desires. He believed that accumulating possessions would bring him happiness."

"One day, a wandering mystic named Yogi Niranjan arrived in the town. Amar, curious about the Yogi's peaceful aura, approached him and asked, 'O revered Yogi, how can I find lasting contentment and peace in the midst of my desires?'"

"Yogi Niranjan smiled gently and replied, 'Desires are like the rivers that flow into the ocean of your consciousness. Seek not to quench them, but to understand their nature.'"

"'The ocean does not resist the rivers,' the Yogi continued, 'and neither should you resist your desires. Observe them without judgment and let them flow through you like the passing clouds in the sky.'"

A light of realization flickered in Maya's eyes as she grasped the essence of the Yogi's wisdom.

Rishi continued, "By recognizing the impermanence of desires and observing them without attachment, you create a space within, like the vastness of the ocean. In this spaciousness, you find inner peace that remains undisturbed by the ebb and flow of desires."

Maya felt a newfound sense of hope and clarity. She realized that true peace did not lie in satisfying desires but in understanding their transient nature.

In the days that followed, Maya practiced the teachings of Rishi, learning to witness her desires without being swept away by them. As she embraced the role of the observer, her mind became a tranquil ocean, undisturbed by the rivers of desires.

And so, the tale of Maya's encounter with the wise sage Rishi became a timeless reminder that one who is not disturbed by the incessant flow of desires, like rivers into the ocean, can indeed achieve lasting peace. Embrace the role of the observer, understand the transient nature of desires, and find inner tranquility in the spacious ocean of consciousness. In this profound stillness lies the true path to contentment and lasting peace amidst life's ever-changing currents.

Taming the Restless Mind

"*The mind is restless and difficult to restrain, but it is subdued by practice.*"
In a serene monastery nestled amidst lush greenery, there lived a revered monk named Swami Sanjay. His eyes exuded a sense of profound serenity, and his presence seemed to calm the turbulent winds of the world.

One day, a young aspirant named Rohan arrived at the monastery, seeking guidance on finding inner peace. He was troubled by the restlessness of his mind, which seemed to veer off in a myriad direction.

Approaching Swami Sanjay with humility, Rohan said, "O revered Swami, my mind is restless, like a wild horse that refuses to be tamed. How can I find stillness amidst the chaos of my thoughts?"

Swami Sanjay smiled gently and beckoned Rohan to sit beside him. "The mind, dear one, is indeed restless and difficult to restrain. But fear not, for it can be subdued through practice."

Intrigued, Rohan asked, "How can I practice subduing the restlessness of my mind?"

Swami Sanjay shared a tale—a timeless story passed down through generations—a tale that held the key to taming the restless mind.

"In a distant village, there lived a determined archer named Arjun. He aspired to master the art of archery, but his mind was as restless as the shifting sands."

"Disheartened by his lack of progress, Arjun sought the counsel of a seasoned archery guru named Guruji. The wise Guruji understood the turbulence of the young archer's mind."

"Upon meeting Arjun, Guruji said, 'The mind is like a powerful steed that needs to be trained. Just as an archer perfects his aim through relentless practice, so can you take your mind through consistent effort.'"

"'Practice the art of concentration,' Guruji continued. 'Focus your mind on a single point, like the tip of an arrow. When the mind wanders, gently guide it back, again and again, until it becomes steady, like a skilled archer's hand.'"

Arjun listened with rapt attention, recognizing the wisdom within Guruji's words.

Swami Sanjay continued, "Dear Rohan, know that taming the restless mind requires practice and patience. Engage in meditation and mindfulness, training your mind to return to the present moment whenever it strays."

"As you persistently practice stillness, you will find the wild waves of thoughts gradually calming. Just as the winds settle in a peaceful valley, so will your mind find tranquility through practice."

Rohan felt a glimmer of hope within his heart as he embraced Swami Sanjay's teachings. He understood that the journey to inner peace required dedication and perseverance.

In the days that followed, Rohan immersed himself in the practice of meditation and mindfulness. Whenever his mind wandered, he gently guided it back to the present moment, like an archer honing his aim.

As weeks turned into months, Rohan noticed a subtle transformation within. His mind, once like a restless horse, began to yield to his gentle guidance. It became more still and centered, like a calm lake reflecting the beauty of the surrounding landscape.

And so, the tale of Rohan's encounter with the revered Swami Sanjay became a timeless reminder that the mind is indeed restless and difficult to restrain. But with practice and perseverance, it can be tamed, just as an archer perfects his aim. Embrace the path of meditation and mindfulness and find the serenity that lies within the depths of a still mind. In this profound stillness, one discovers the true essence of inner peace.

Surrendering to the Divine Flow

"The power of God is with you at all times; through the activities of mind, senses, breathing, and emotions; and is constantly doing all the work using you as a mere instrument."

In a tranquil ashram nestled amidst the verdant hills, lived a wise sage named Guru Dev. His eyes held a profound light that seemed to reflect the very essence of divinity.

One day, a seeker named Aanya arrived at the ashram, seeking solace and spiritual guidance. She yearned to understand the mysteries of life and the presence of the divine in every moment.

Approaching Guru Dev with reverence, Aanya said, "O revered Guru Dev, I often wonder about the power of God and how it works through us. How can I align myself with this divine force and find meaning in my actions?"

Guru Dev smiled; his face radiant with compassion. "Dear Aanya, the power of God is indeed with you at all times. It flows through the activities of your mind, senses, breathing, and emotions. You are a mere instrument through which this divine force works its magic."

Intrigued, Aanya asked, "But how can I surrender to this divine flow and allow it to guide my actions?"

Guru Dev shared a tale—a timeless story that carried the essence of surrendering to the divine flow of life.

"In a bustling city, there lived a talented painter named Kavya. Her brushstrokes created masterpieces that seemed to come alive on the canvas. Yet, beneath her artistic brilliance, she yearned for a deeper purpose in her creations."

"One day, a renowned art teacher named Maestro Rajan visited the city. Sensing Kavya's restlessness, he approached her and said, 'Dear Kavya, the divine flow of creativity resides within you. Surrender to this force and let it guide your artistic expression.'"

"Kavya was intrigued and asked, 'But how can I surrender to this divine flow and find meaning in my art?'"

"Maestro Rajan replied, 'The key lies in letting go of the ego, the belief that your art is separate from the divine. When you paint with humility, knowing that you are an instrument of a greater force, your creations become imbued with a profound essence.'"

Aanya listened with rapt attention, feeling the resonance of the tale within her heart.

Guru Dev continued, "Dear Aanya, surrendering to the divine flow requires letting go of the illusion of control and ego. When you act with love, compassion, and selflessness, you become an instrument of the divine force, which works through you."

"The power of God is ever-present, guiding your thoughts, actions, and emotions. Embrace each moment with gratitude and trust in the divine plan. Let go of the burden of personal desires and allow the divine flow to weave its magic through your life."

Aanya felt a deep sense of peace as she absorbed Guru Dev's teachings. She realized that by surrendering to the divine force, she could find true purpose and meaning in her journey.

In the days that followed, Aanya practiced surrendering to the divine flow, offering her actions as a loving tribute to the greater force that worked through her.

With each passing day, she felt a profound connection to the universe, knowing that she was but a vessel through which the divine power manifested its infinite expressions.

And so, the tale of Aanya's encounter with the wise Guru Dev became a timeless reminder that the power of God is always indeed with us. Embrace each moment with surrender, allowing the divine flow to guide your thoughts, senses, and emotions. In this sacred union with the divine, you become a vessel of love and purpose, contributing to the greater harmony of existence.

The Journey of Impermanence

"*You came empty-handed, and you will leave empty-handed.*"
In a remote village, where time seemed to stand still, lived a venerable elder named Grandma Meera. Her eyes held a depth of wisdom that came with the passing of countless seasons.

One evening, as the sun dipped below the horizon, a young traveler named Ravi arrived at Grandma Meera's humble abode. He was on a quest to understand the mysteries of life and the true essence of existence.

Approaching Grandma Meera with a sense of awe, Ravi said, "O wise Grandma, life feels fleeting, and possessions seem temporary. What is the purpose of our journey when everything is left behind in the end?"

Grandma Meera smiled gently, a knowing twinkle in her eyes. "Dear one," she replied, "you came empty-handed into this world, and you will leave empty-handed. The journey of life is an impermanent dance, and its true purpose lies beyond material possessions."

Intrigued, Ravi asked, "But how can I find meaning in a world that appears so transient?"

Grandma Meera shared a tale—a timeless story that carried the essence of life's impermanence.

"In a lush valley, there lived a contented farmer named Govind. He worked the fertile soil with love, tending to his crops with care. Despite his modest possessions, he radiated a sense of inner peace and abundance."

"One day, a wandering philosopher named Sage Nanda arrived in the village. Intrigued by Govind's peaceful aura, she approached him and said, 'O noble farmer, how do you find contentment when everything seems so ephemeral?'"

"Govind smiled warmly and replied, 'I understand that life is but a fleeting journey, and possessions are mere companions along the way. What truly matters is the love we share, the kindness we offer, and the memories we create.'"

"Sage Nanda nodded, recognizing the profound wisdom in Govind's words."

Grandma Meera continued, "Dear Ravi, the purpose of life transcends the accumulation of possessions. It lies in the richness of experiences, the connections we foster, and the legacy of love we leave behind."

"Understand that all material wealth is temporary, but the impact you have on others' lives can leave an eternal imprint. Embrace the journey of impermanence with grace, cherishing every moment, and valuing the relationships that fill your heart."

Ravi felt a sense of clarity settling within his soul. He understood that life's true essence lay in embracing its impermanence and finding meaning beyond the confines of material possessions.

In the days that followed, Ravi journeyed with a newfound perspective. He treasured each encounter and moment, cherishing the gift of impermanence that lent depth and significance to every experience.

And so, the tale of Ravi's encounter with the venerable Grandma Meera became a timeless reminder that we come empty-handed into this world and leave empty-handed. Embrace life's impermanence with gratitude, for it grants us the opportunity to cherish precious moments, build meaningful connections, and leave a legacy of love. In this profound embrace of impermanence lies the true essence of our journey.

The Path of Devotion and Mindful Mastery

"*A person cannot achieve devotion without controlling their mind.*"

In the heart of a bustling city, amidst the cacophony of daily life, lived a devout seeker named Maya. Her heart yearned for a deep connection with the divine, seeking solace amidst the whirlwind of thoughts and emotions.

One day, as Maya sat in quiet contemplation by the river, a wise sage named Swami Devendra approached her. His eyes exuded a profound tranquility that seemed to mirror the depths of the universe.

Approaching Maya with a gentle smile, Swami Devendra said, "O seeker of truth, devotion to the divine is a sacred journey. But to tread this path, one must first learn to control the restless waves of the mind."

Intrigued, Maya asked, "But how can I achieve devotion while my mind seems to wander endlessly?"

Swami Devendra shared a tale—a timeless story woven with the wisdom of mindful mastery.

"In a distant village, there lived a devoted young musician named Veena. Her heart poured into every melody she played, seeking to offer her music as a tribute to the divine."

"One day, a revered music teacher named Guruji arrived in the village. Sensing Veena's sincerity, he approached her and said, 'Dear Veena, the art of devotion lies not only in your music but in the mastery of your mind.'"

"Veena was intrigued and asked, 'How can I attain control over my mind and deepen my devotion?'"

"Guruji replied, 'Practice the art of mindfulness—become the observer of your thoughts, emotions, and desires. As you learn to detach from the mind's restlessness, you will uncover the tranquil lake of devotion within.'"

Maya absorbed Swami Devendra's words, sensing the essence of mindfulness in the path of devotion.

Swami Devendra continued, "Dear Maya, devotion is like a fragrant flower that blooms in the garden of a still mind. Through meditation and mindfulness, cultivate the ability to direct your thoughts towards the divine. Offer your heart's devotion like a river merging into the ocean of divine love."

"With a focused mind, your devotion becomes a pure offering—free from the ripples of distraction. Embrace each moment with awareness, and your connection with the divine will deepen beyond measure."

Maya felt a profound shift within her soul. She understood that mindfulness was the key to unlocking the depths of devotion she sought.

In the days that followed, Maya embraced the teachings of Swami Devendra, practicing meditation and mindfulness. With each breath, she learned to navigate the labyrinth of her thoughts, gently steering them towards the divine.

As her mind became more tranquil, her devotion blossomed like a radiant flower, suffusing her heart with divine love.

And so, the tale of Maya's encounter with the wise Swami Devendra became a timeless reminder that a person cannot achieve devotion without controlling their mind. Embrace the path of mindfulness and mindful mastery, for it opens the gateway to a heart overflowing with devotion. In the stillness of the mind lies the sacred dance of devotion—a journey that leads to the divine embrace of eternal love.

The Serenity of Detached Duty

*"**P**erform your duty with a calm mind, without attachment to success or failure."*

In a quaint village nestled amidst rolling hills, lived a skilled artisan named Arjun. With meticulous craftsmanship, he created exquisite pottery that adorned the homes of villagers far and wide.

One day, as they sunbathed the village in golden hues, a curious young villager named Kavya approached Arjun. Intrigued by his serene aura, she asked, "O respected Arjun, how do you craft such beautiful pottery with such calmness and finesse?"

Arjun smiled warmly and replied, "Dear Kavya, the secret lies in performing my duty with a calm mind, without attachment to success or failure."

Intrigued, Kavya asked, "But how do you remain detached when your artistry is admired by all?"

Arjun shared a tale—a timeless story that echoed the essence of detached duty.

"In a bustling city, there lived a talented musician named Amar. His melodic tunes touched the hearts of all who listened. Yet, within him, a sense of restlessness simmered, yearning for constant validation and applause."

"One day, a wise sage named Sageesh visited the city. Sensing Amar's inner turmoil, he approached the musician and said, 'O skilled artist, find solace in performing your duty without attachment. Embrace your passion for music, but do not let the outcomes dictate your happiness.'"

A spark of understanding flickered in Kavya's eyes as she grasped the essence of Arjun's wisdom.

Arjun continued, "Dear Kavya, performing your duty with a calm mind means giving your utmost without being entangled in the fruits of your labor. Embrace each moment of creativity and craftsmanship with love and dedication but let go of any attachment to praise or success."

Kavya felt a sense of resonance with Arjun's teachings, realizing the significance of detached duty in finding inner peace.

Arjun continued, "When we are detached, success and failure lose their power to sway us. The mind becomes a tranquil lake, reflecting the beauty of the present moment. Detachment empowers us to remain focused on the process, leading to mastery and fulfillment in our endeavors."

In the days that followed, Kavya observed Arjun as he crafted pottery with a serene demeanor. He immersed himself in each stroke of the brush, in every sculpting of clay, finding joy in the act of creation itself.

Inspired, Kavya began to apply Arjun's teachings in her own life. She pursued her interests and duties with a calm mind, savoring the journey without being enslaved by the outcomes.

And so, the tale of Arjun's encounter with the curious young villager, Kavya, became a timeless reminder that performing your duty with a calm mind and detached heart leads to true fulfillment. Embrace each task with love and dedication, unburdened by attachment to success or failure. In this serene dance of detached duty, you find inner peace and joy that transcends the fleeting whispers of the world.

The Battle of the Restless Mind

"*The mind is restless, turbulent, obstinate, and very strong, O Krishna, and to subdue it, I think, is more difficult than controlling the wind.*"

In the sacred land of Kurukshetra, where the echoes of wisdom resounded, stood Arjuna, a valiant warrior, and Krishna, the divine charioteer and guide.

As they prepared for the great battle of life, Arjuna, troubled by the tumultuous thoughts that stirred within him, turned to Krishna and said, "O Krishna, the mind is restless, turbulent, obstinate, and very strong. To subdue it, I believe, is more difficult than controlling the wind."

Krishna listened with profound understanding, a gentle smile playing upon his lips. "Indeed, Arjuna," he replied, "the mind is a relentless force, prone to wandering and entangled in desires. But fear not, for it can be mastered through discipline and practice."

With compassionate eyes, Krishna began to share a tale—a timeless story that echoed the battle of the restless mind.

"In a distant kingdom, there lived a skilled archer named Arun. He was celebrated for his prowess, yet within him raged a constant struggle to tame the wild currents of his thoughts."

"Feeling disheartened, Arun sought the counsel of a revered yogi named Guruji. The wise Guruji understood the storms that raged within the archer's mind."

Upon meeting Arun, Guruji said, "Dear Arun, the mind is indeed like a tempestuous sea. But just as a skilled captain navigates turbulent waters with mastery, so can you harness your mind through unwavering practice."

Intrigued, Arun asked, "But how can I gain control over my restless mind, O revered Guruji?"

Guruji replied, "Through meditation and self-awareness, embrace your thoughts without judgment or resistance. Let them come and go like passing clouds in the vast expanse of the sky."

"By observing the mind's restlessness, you disentangle yourself from its grasp. Cultivate detachment, and the mind's obstinacy will gradually subside, like a storm that yields to a serene sky."

As Krishna concluded the tale, Arjuna felt a glimmer of hope, understanding that the mind could indeed be tamed through practice and discipline.

Krishna reassured him, "Dear Arjuna, the mind's restlessness can be conquered through perseverance and devotion. Embrace meditation, self-awareness, and the path of selfless action. As you do so, you will find the stillness and strength within you to face life's challenges with grace."

In the days that followed, Arjuna immersed himself in Krishna's teachings, learning to observe his restless mind with detachment. Through meditation and mindful practice, he began to tame the turbulent waves of thoughts, finding solace in the depths of his being.

And so, the tale of Arjuna's contemplation with Krishna on the battlefield of life became a timeless reminder that the mind is indeed restless, but with dedicated practice and devotion, it can be subdued. Embrace meditation and self-awareness, for they are the keys to mastering the mind's turbulent currents. Just as a skilled warrior wields his bow with precision, so you can navigate the battlefield of your mind with unwavering focus and serenity.

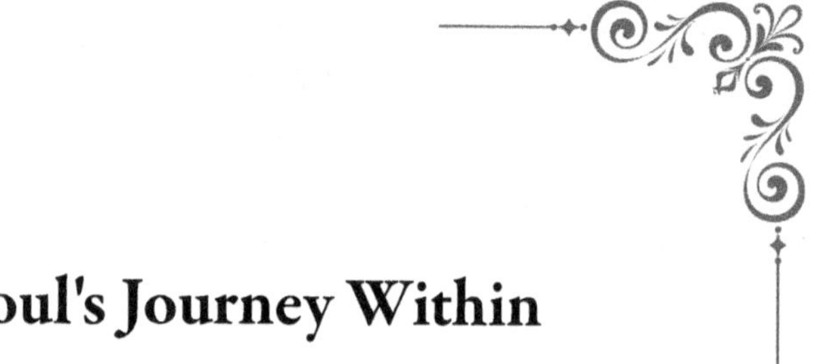

The Soul's Journey Within

"*The soul who meditates on the Self is content to serve the Self and rests satisfied within the Self.*"

In the ancient land of sacred teachings, a revered sage named Rishi Veda resided atop a serene mountain. Seekers from far and wide would make the arduous journey to seek his wisdom and guidance.

One day, a curious seeker named Anika arrived at Rishi Veda's abode, her heart yearning to unravel the mysteries of the Self. With a humble bow, she asked, "O wise sage, how can I find contentment and inner peace within myself?"

Rishi Veda smiled, his eyes reflecting the depth of his knowledge. "Dear seeker," he replied, "contentment arises when the soul turns inward to meditate on the Self. By serving the Self, one discovers true satisfaction and tranquility."

Intrigued, Anika asked, "But what is the nature of this Self that I must serve?"

Rishi Veda began to share a tale—a timeless story steeped in the essence of self-discovery.

"In a distant village, there lived a gentle-hearted farmer named Sanjay. His days were spent toiling in the fields, but within him, a longing for deeper meaning stirred."

"One day, while tending to his crops, Sanjay encountered a revered mystic named Guruji. The sage's serene presence drew Sanjay like a moth to a flame."

Sanjay approached Guruji with humility and asked, "O revered Guruji, how can I find contentment and fulfillment in my life?"

Guruji replied, "Contentment is not found in external pursuits alone, but through the journey within. Meditate on the Self—the essence that resides within you—and discover the infinite wellspring of peace and fulfillment."

Sanjay pondered Guruji's words, realizing that the path to contentment lay within himself.

Rishi Veda continued, "Dear Anika, when the soul turns inward to meditate on the Self, it discovers its true nature—a boundless source of joy and contentment. By serving the Self, one finds solace and satisfaction beyond the ephemeral pursuits of the world."

Anika felt a profound resonance with Rishi Veda's teachings, understanding that true contentment was a journey of self-discovery.

In the days that followed, Anika immersed herself in the practice of meditation and self-inquiry. As she delved deeper into the recesses of her being, she found a wellspring of peace and fulfillment within the depths of her soul.

And so, the tale of Anika's encounter with the revered sage Rishi Veda became a timeless reminder that contentment is found within oneself. Meditate on the Self, and you will uncover the eternal source of joy and peace that rests within the soul. By serving the Self, you find solace and satisfaction that transcends the transient pursuits of the world. Embrace the journey within, and you will discover the boundless treasure of contentment that has been with you all along.

About the Author

Jignesh, a devoted project engineer during the day and an ardent writer at heart, possesses a unique blend of analytical prowess and creative finesse. His insatiable **love for storytelling** fuels his mission to unravel intricate topics in a way that captivates readers and makes learning an enchanting experience.

With a canvas of words, Jignesh weaves tales that bridge the chasm between complex concepts and everyday life, creating literary tapestries that entwine the profound with the practical. He believes in the power of storytelling to unlock the doors of understanding, inviting readers of all backgrounds to embark on a journey of knowledge and self-discovery.

Beyond the world of engineering, Jignesh's soul finds solace in the realm of literature and the art of expression. Each sentence he pens is crafted with passion and purpose, driven by the conviction that education should be an enjoyable voyage of curiosity and wonder.

When he is not immersed in the realm of storytelling, Jignesh can be found communing with nature's beauty, penning verses of poetry, or sharing cherished moments with loved ones. His unwavering commitment to both his professional career and creative pursuits reflects a harmonious balance between the logical and the imaginative.

www.ingramcontent.com/pod-product-compliance
Lightning Source LLC
Chambersburg PA
CBHW050548160726
48003CB00002B/804